Your Friend

THE VALUE OF
FRIENDSHIP FOR A LIFETIME

MICHAEL W. SMITH

with GARY THOMAS

THOMAS NELSON PUBLISHERS®
Nashville

Published in Nashville, Tennessee, by Thomas Nelson, Inc.

Library of Congress Cataloging-in-Publication Data

ISBN 0-7852-7036-1
Control Number: 2001 130181

Printed in the United States of America

2 3 4 5 6 7 8 9 10 QW 06 05 04 03 02 01

In one of the greatest movies of all times,
It's a Wonderful Life, George Bailey
(Jimmy Stewart) is reminded that
"no man is a failure who has friends"

I couldn't attempt to say it any better.
I am a blessed man—not by any material thing I
own or have achieved. I am so because of the
friends I have. I am thankful for them all and it is
to my friends that I dedicate this book.

Contents

I Will Be Your Friend

So many memories, so many miles
The road that stretches behind us;
We've had some laughter and our share of tears
But all these moments unite us.

I'll be your friend for a lifetime
Against the wind and rain of every season;
Won't walk away in the hard times—
I will be your friend,
I will be your friend.

Sure as the river runs to the sea,
High as the mountain that reaches,
You were there by my side till the end
(and) helped me on my feet again.

I'll be your friend for a lifetime
Against the wind and rain of every season;
Won't walk away in the hard times—
I will be your friend,
I will be your friend.

So in the valley, walk on—
Don't have to face it alone
'Cause in the hard times
We keep growing strong
And we learn as we live
That we live when we give.

CHAPTER ONE

Why Bother with Friends?

$\mathcal{A}$t the age of fourteen, like most teenagers, I craved attention and never got enough to satisfy my soul. Nobody really picked on me; it was more the case that too few people noticed me. When you're that age, sometimes the worst thing people can do to you is to ignore you.

When I tried to step out of my insecurity, I frequently got slammed. One time, I asked a girl out on a date. She was without a doubt the most gorgeous young woman I had ever seen. We went to a skating rink, holding hands during the pairs skating, and even her hand felt incredibly wonderful. The whole night, I went out of my way to treat her with respect and to help her have a good time.

Near the end of the date, I was consumed with the choice, Do I kiss her or not? I decided not to push it. We said good night and I walked home thinking it was one of the best times of my life. I couldn't wait to get together again.

I called her the next day, and my heart fell as soon as I heard her voice. You just know when the excitement isn't there and when the other person doesn't share your feelings. I could read from her tone that my call was an intrusion. By the time I asked, "Would you like to do something tonight?" I knew it was hopeless.

"I've got other plans," she said, without any emotion and without any encouragement to ask her again some other time.

I knew it was over.

2

I can still remember putting down the phone, and all the thoughts that ran through my head. *Is it my hair? Don't I look good enough? Do I smell? What could I have done differently? Wasn't I polite?*

Now that I have kids older than fourteen, my perspective has changed a little bit. Sometimes, two people just don't click. Back then, that was a little harder for me to accept.

Like just about everyone else who's gone through adolescence, I struggled with this sense of whether I really "belonged" off and on throughout high school, never really pulling out of it. It wasn't until much later in my life that I finally woke up and thought, *You know what? I'm okay.*

Fast-forward twenty years, to my high school reunion. My success in contemporary Christian music as well as in the pop field had opened up a lot of doors for me. When I walked into the reunion, lots of people couldn't wait to talk to me.

"Hey, Michael, I saw you on the Grammys! Congratulations!"

"Smitty! It was great seeing you on the American Music Awards."

All night long, I kept thinking how interesting

it is—the tide really does turn. Now, plenty of people wanted to hang with me. Back then, there were always those times when I wondered if I could even *buy* a friend.

Though I carried my share of hurt in high school, I also did my share of hurting others. One friend—a girl I dated in high school, whom I hadn't seen in almost ten years—came backstage after a concert. It was a shock to see her, but more than that, I was taken aback by the way she glared at me as soon as she caught my eye. After all, if you haven't seen a friend in a long time, you usually say something nice. Instead, she blurted out, "You hurt me. You really hurt me. You broke my heart."

I didn't know what to say. "I'm sorry," I offered. "I'm just so, so sorry."

Friendships—good and bad—have been a major part of my life. I've lived through times when friends came hard, and I've lived through times when friends came easy. I've shared some of the best times in my life with friends, but I've also been hurt by friends—both intentionally and unintentionally. More recently, I've lost a couple of close friends—author Bob Briner, from Hollywood, and

4

Carol Ann Lee, part of our prayer group, just to
name two.

Friendships have had a major impact on my
faith. I agree with Paul Stevens, a seminary professor, who writes, "Unquestionably my primary theological education has been from *people,* not books
or classes. And the history of my own spiritual life
is substantially the history of my relationships."[1]

Think about that for a minute. Here's a guy
who has all the degrees, who in fact is on the fac-
ulty of a seminary and who has served as an aca-
demic dean, but who still believes that he has
learned more from his friendships than from
books. Stevens explains, "Relational life is not a
mere accessory to spirituality or ministry, but the
heart of it."[2] He goes on to write:

> The word *together* appears so frequently in Paul's
> writings that it deserves special study. Paul uses the
> Greek prefix *sun* ("with" or "together") and joins
> this prefix to a number of key words to describe
> the practical impossibility of being in Christ alone.
> What is translated into English as a phrase is one
> compound word in the original: "fellow citizens"

(Eph. 2:19); "fitted together" (2:21); "being built together" (2:22); and, reaching a climax, "joined and knit together by what every joint supplies" (4:16). Paul is using the strongest possible language—indeed he is creating new language—to describe the interdependence of every member of the body. We can no more disconnect ourselves from other members and remain healthy than we can disconnect the ligaments from the bones or try to live without veins or arteries.[3]

In this book, I want to walk with you through the land of friendships; discussing how important they are, how to have better friendships, and how to fix the ones that have gone bad. I guess I agree with Francis Schaeffer, who wrote, "We must all measure ourselves by our friendships—apart from the Scriptures, there is no surer measure to be had in this poor fallen world."[4]

What Is a Friend?

What makes someone a friend? When is that mystical moment that an acquaintance becomes something more? We pass hundreds, maybe even thousands of people a day, yet only a very few get pegged as friends. At our churches, we rub shoulders with dozens of other members, but only have lunch or dinner with a very few.

Why is that? What makes someone a friend?

Jerry and Mary White, authors of *Friends & Friendship*, define a friend this way: "A friend is a trusted confidant to whom I am mutually drawn as a companion and an ally, whose love for me is not dependent on my performance, and whose influence draws me closer to God."[5]

I think a friend is someone you really care about and with whom you have something in common. A friend cares for you, without any conditions and without any ulterior motives. A true friend doesn't care what I've done or where I've been; there's an unconditional commitment that will never die.

When I think of a true friend, I think of Don Finto, my pastor and mentor for over twenty years, who frequently calls me and leaves a message that goes something like this, "Michael, I love you. You're a godly man. Stay strong. Stay plugged in. Don't let the enemy get a foothold." These little encouraging messages show me that Don isn't in a relationship with me because he wants something from me; he calls because he cares, period.

The Whites have identified eight qualities that they think characterize most friends. According to them, a friend is someone who is loyal, shares deeply, is fun to be around, and is stimulating, encouraging, loving, spiritually challenging, and self-sacrificing.

I think that's a pretty good list, and all of these characteristics will be discussed later in this book. For now, I want you to think about what friendship means to you. When you hear the word *friend*, does it make you feel angry or happy? Maybe friendship comes hard to you; perhaps it's full of hurt, and you don't even like to talk about it. Or maybe just the word *friendship* makes you feel warm inside. You've got a lot of great friendships and a ton of good memories.

We can exist without friendships, but I'm not sure we can truly *live* without them. C. S. Lewis once wrote, "Friendship is unnecessary, like philosophy, like art. It has no survival value; rather it is one of those things that give value to survival."[6] I agree with Lewis; everything I've done in this life wouldn't matter much at all if I didn't have friends to share it with.

There are some life situations that virtually require friends locking arms. Stu Weber explains in his book by that title:

> Just imagine a large car stuck in the sand. When one man puts his back and leg strength against the rear end of the car, nothing happens. Two men might rock it forward a little. But three men pushing together feel the weight yield, and the tires claw out of the hole. Three men get the car out of the ditch and back on the road. Some of us have been straining against immovable problems and dug-in frustrations for a long time. Every day we push and shove, grit our teeth and dig in our heels, but the mass doesn't budge. Nothing seems to change. Could it be that our good God might be *allowing* these very kinds of situations in our lives to help us learn an elemental truth? Some loads need more than a lone man's strength. Some problems won't budge until two or three friends put their shoulders into it.
>
> Together. God's way, every time.[7]

Do you have some friends who will lock arms

with you? Whatever places you're coming from, I hope this book will help you make friendships even more of a priority in your life.

A LIFE THEME

Friendship has definitely been one of the main themes of my music. One of the most popular songs that I've recorded—the song I think most defines me to this day—is "Friends," written back in 1982, before I had released my first album. I was still making a living just by writing songs, and Debbie and I were barely making it financially, living in a small duplex on the west side of Nashville.

We had a small group that met for Bible study and worship every Sunday night that became pretty tight. One of the members, Bill Jackson, announced that he was moving to Auburn to work with the Fellowship of Christian Athletes, one of Campus Crusade's ministries. We were happy for Bill, believing it was a good move for him and a clear case of God's calling, but saddened that he wouldn't be with us anymore.

On the afternoon of the last Sunday Bill would

be with us, Debbie came up with the crazy idea of writing a song for him.

"That's not gonna work," I protested. "You don't write songs that way. The Bible study is two hours from now. How are we going to write a song before then?"

Instead of sitting down at the piano, I went outside and played with our dog. It couldn't have been more than fifteen minutes later when I came back inside. Deb met me at the door and showed me a sheet of lyrics. I read them and could not believe it. I was shocked. What an amazing lyric.

Even so, a lyric without music is called poetry, not a song. I had just one hour and forty-five minutes to find a melody. As it turned out, I didn't need to worry; the tune came in about five minutes.

I played it for Bill that night, and the tears flowed. I really liked the song, so I decided to pitch it to Amy Grant. I played it for Mike Blanton, our manager at the time, and he loved it. As we rode up in an elevator on our way to Mike's office, I asked, "Don't you think this song would be great for Amy?"

Mike surprised me by shaking his head and saying, "*You* need to cut this song."

"You really think so?"

"Yes, I do."

I'm glad Mike held the line on this one. "Friends" is still probably the most popular thing I've ever done.

As we laid out the songs that would be included on the *This Is Your Time* CD, I knew friendship would be another theme. After all, it was Cassie Bernall's friendship with Jesus that led her to lay down her life rather than deny her best friend when cornered by the Columbine killers.

IT IS NOT GOOD

Some people might ask, If we really love God, do we still need friends?

Absolutely.

Remember, it was God Himself who said to Adam, "It is not good that man should be alone; I will make him a helper comparable to him" (Gen. 2:18). Even in paradise, when Adam had everything he needed and a close walk with the Creator, God Himself thought Adam needed a friend.

Our love for each other—our desire for deep friendship—doesn't conflict with our desire for God. It's part of it! That's what Dietrich Bonhoeffer meant when he wrote, "The believer feels no shame, as though he were still living too much in the flesh, when he yearns for the physical presence of other Christians. Man was created a body, the Son of God appeared on earth in the body, he was raised in the body, in the sacrament the believer receives the Lord Christ in the body, and the resurrection of the dead will bring about the perfected fellowship of God's spiritual-physical creatures. The believer therefore lauds the Creator, the Redeemer, God, Father, Son and Holy Spirit, for the bodily presence of a brother."[8]

Friends don't get in the way of our walk with God; in fact, they help make God more real to us. They comfort us in the difficult times and celebrate with us in the good times. Friends make life worth living.

Friends are what it's all about.

CHAPTER TWO

Friends in Tough Times

In 1993, a large group of U.S. Army Rangers performed a routine sweep into Mogadishu, Somalia, to round up some troublesome elements. Everything was going as planned until approximately thirty-five minutes into the operation when the lead Blackhawk helicopter was shot down by a rocket-propelled grenade. Other Blackhawks were following, and it wouldn't have been too difficult for the Rangers to cut their losses and run, but instead they did what seemed to outsiders a "curious" thing. One hundred soldiers encircled the downed helicopter in a desperate attempt to retrieve the dead pilot's body.

The other men in the damaged aircraft had already been rescued, so newspaper reporters wanted to know why so many soldiers put their lives in jeopardy to retrieve a dead man's body, pointing out that there is no Army requirement to do so.

In his book *Locking Arms,* Stu Weber, a Christian pastor and former Army Ranger, sheds some light on what happened. During Ranger training, you're paired up with a buddy. The non-com who trained Weber at Ft. Benning explained, "Difficult assignments require a friend. The two of you will stick together. You will never leave each other. You will walk together, run together, eat together, sleep together. You will help each other. You will encourage each other. And, as necessary, you will carry each other."[1]

The Rangers learned early on that survival depended on being faithful to your friend. There would come a time when your life might depend on this buddy; it was not a relationship to be taken lightly.

"We got the point," Stu explains. It was the Army's way of saying, 'Never go into the water alone. Never go into battle alone. Never, ever walk alone. Stay together, Rangers! Live together . . . and if necessary, die together.'"[2]

While the newspaper reporters wanted to know why men risked their lives for a dead comrade (eighteen soldiers were killed and seventy-five were wounded in this action), Army personnel explained that Rangers live by their own creed, to "complete the mission, though I be the lone survivor" and never to "leave a fallen comrade to fall into the hands of the enemy."

Stu reflects on this incident and writes, "Now I ask you, which kind of a friend would you want? One that cuts and runs at the first sign of real trouble? Or one that will stay with you no matter what? In the heat of the intense, hectic, chaos of combat, who has the time to fully and instantaneously measure the difference between a seriously wounded, unconscious body and one from which

life has departed? And if there is *any* doubt what-
soever (and you were that body) what would you
want your friends to do? There is no doubt in my
mind. There is no greater love than that a man lay
down his life for his friends."[3]

Weber warns that the loftiest value in America
today is self: "Self-orientation. Self-improvement.
Self-preservation. Self-assertion." He calls our
"Cult of the Individual" the most destructive and
insidious false religion in this country. Against this
backdrop, we need to paint a new picture of
friendship that will deny self and be loyal to the
end.

A FRIEND IN NEED

Friendship brings a lot of rewards, but there are
also the seasons when having friends brings pain,
confusion, hurt, and even anger into your life.
That's really the story behind the song "I Will Be
Your Friend." A number of our friends were going
through some very difficult, even mind-boggling
stuff. One was questioning his faith; one was walking away from the Lord; a couple was getting a

divorce; yet another was launching himself into an entirely different "lifestyle."

A close friend was battling unemployment and financial quicksand, getting buried deeper every week, each new bill sinking him and his wife just a few more inches into a bottomless pit. He confessed to me how the financial pressure was affecting his home life. Fights, disagreements, and frustration were building every day.

"It's high drama, man," he said. "I feel like I'm on the verge of losing it."

What do you do when your friends—the people you care about most in the world—go through such difficult times? I couldn't "fix" anything. I could listen to them, but I couldn't put their marriage back together. I couldn't offer a job, or wave a wand over their heads to erase their "identity" problems.

I realized all I could do was to be there for them. I told some of them outright, "I'll never cease to be your friend. I don't care where you go, or what's going on in your head—I'll stand in the gap for you; I'll be your friend for a lifetime."

Friend for a lifetime . . .

Those words kind of stuck. I really believed they had flowed out of my mouth for a reason, so I sat down and started to write. I wrote the music and title for "I Will Be Your Friend" in about five minutes. It was just one of those things. I then called on Cindy Morgan to finish the lyrics, for two reasons: she's a great writer, and she's fast. A lot of times, these decisions—whom to send a song to—are often based on nothing more than a gut feeling. You just go with what you know is right, and I knew Cindy was the one to write this song.

I was right. She did a great job. As I read the finished product, I was reminded of one time when I wasn't the friend I needed to be—and the tragedy that followed.

One Missed Phone Call

Back in the early eighties, I lived in Nashville near Dale, a friend from my hometown. Dale was a good friend and very talented artistically, but he was a very complicated guy. He loved the Lord, yet battled some pretty serious emotional problems most of his life.

At times, I had trouble communicating with him. I tried to "stand in the gap" and help him through some tough times, but there was one night when the talk got a little heated. Dale was having a difficult time financially and personally. He told me he planned on getting a divorce, and I begged him to give his marriage another chance, but he didn't want to hear it.

It wasn't the best time for me, either. I was still struggling to make it in Nashville. I had just signed my first songwriting contract, but it paid something like $200 a week, so I certainly wasn't rolling in the money. And though I had rededicated my life to the Lord, I was in the midst of a couple of rough months. So, after Dale hung up on me, I decided to go on with my plans for the evening and call him the next day.

I came back late and fell into bed. A few hours later, my phone rang. It was my mom, telling me that Dale's parents had just received a call telling them their son had committed suicide.

"Say that again, Mom," I begged. "That can't be right!"

I was in shock. I threw on my clothes and drove

over to Dale's place, his roommates confirmed my mom's report. I got back into my car and drove to the hospital. They wouldn't give me a whole lot of information. All I knew was that Dale was dead. He had hanged himself.

It was up to me to call his mom and dad back and tell them everything I knew. I went to Dale's apartment and started packing up his stuff, then dropped a suit off at the dry cleaners for the burial.

It felt like I was drifting in the twilight zone. None of this seemed real or possible.

I drove to West Virginia, my car crammed with Dale's stuff. It was a long drive, and every mile, I wrestled with the thoughts, *I blew it. I really blew it. It's all my fault. If I had called Dale back right away, this might not have happened.*

At home in West Virginia, Dale's parents, my parents, and a lot of friends did all they could to talk me out of my guilt. "This has been going on for a long time, Michael," they said. "It's not your fault."

It took a while for me to agree with them. Looking back today, I know I stood by Dale for years. I spent many nights trying to convince him that taking his own life was not the answer. Surely I could convey the depth of God's love for Dale, and I had helped talk him through many rough stretches. But in the end, there was probably nothing more I could have done.

Still, his suicide really hit me hard. At Dale's funeral I decided that in the future, I was going to be the best friend I could be. What I didn't realize at that time was how many chances I would get to keep living out this commitment.

REPUTATION AT RISK

Recently, I performed at a show that featured two close friends, both of whom had gone through some pretty public divorces. It was a great show, and I think a lot of people were touched, but the flak immediately started flying.

I could almost hear the comments:

"Michael, you're condoning divorce!"

"So, Smitty, I guess staying married really doesn't mean that much to you, does it?"

Even more hurtful things were shared and expressed that I won't mention here. The fact is, I hate it when *any* marriage fails. I've seen what divorce does to kids, and I'm more committed than ever to making my marriage with Deb last for a lifetime. But does that mean I'm going to dump every friend who gets a divorce?

Think about it: Should I stop performing with anyone who confesses to occasional struggles with pornography or other addictions? Am I going to refuse to associate with someone who has temper tantrums or cheats at golf? With this standard, it wouldn't be long before I'd run out of friends—and before everybody else would have to dump me as a friend too.

The people criticizing me had no idea what I had shared or hadn't shared with my friends. They didn't have a clue about what happened behind the scenes, but it's not my intention to defend myself here. Let's take a look at the big picture. Let's ask ourselves: Are we fair-weather friends? Will we hang around only with seemingly perfect people? If a friend does something we disagree with, does that mean the friendship has to come to an end?

I hope not. Proverbs says, "A friend loves at all times, and a brother is born for adversity" (Prov.

17:17). The same writer adds, "There is a friend who sticks closer than a brother" (Prov. 18:24).

I want to be that kind of friend, the kind portrayed in the next story.

"I Knew It"

Stu Weber recounts a well-known story coming out of World War I. In an American trench, a deep friendship was born between two soldiers. There was a lot of downtime, and then moments of sheer terror as each side climbed out of their trenches and attacked the other. Between battles, the two men talked about their dreams and shared their fears. As the conflict continued to erupt and they faced death again and again, they grew especially close.

One night they left the trench to stage another attack. During that fight, one of the men received a severe wound. When the other made it back to the trench and discovered that his friend was lying somewhere outside, bleeding, he decided to go after him.

Since the shelling was still going on, the officer in charge forbade the guy to leave the trench. "Too dangerous." he said. "It's not worth the risk." When the officer turned his head, the soldier crawled out anyway. He endured the ear-splitting concussion of the shells, choked on the smoke, and braved the bullets until he reached his friend, then slowly dragged him back into the trench.

There the rescuer found that his wounded buddy had died along the way. The officer, upset that his order had been disobeyed, challenged the soldier. "So, was it worth the risk?"

"Yes sir, it was," he replied. "My friend's last words made it more than worth it. He looked up at me and said, 'I knew you'd come.'"[4]

When your friends really need you, will you be there for them? Are you willing to put your own life on the line, just to hear the words, "I knew you'd come"?

CHAPTER THREE

Choosing Friends

I came to appreciate friends early on. One of my first good friends was Joe Dorsey, our school quarterback, who topped out at about 5′9″—maybe the smallest passer I have ever seen. We lived half a block away from each other, but our common bond was sports. I probably spent more hours with Joe than with anyone else when I was growing up.

Life has a way of pulling friends apart, though. I moved from West Virginia to Nashville to try to make it in the music business; Joe took a job at an oil refinery. Vocationally, our worlds couldn't have been more distant, and living several states away, it wasn't like we could meet for lunch.

We lost contact, until one time when I went to Cincinatti, Ohio, to play a concert at Riverfront Stadium after the Reds game. Because I was close to my hometown, a lot of high school friends came to the show. We had a big, backstage reunion, and I was amazed at how much everybody had changed. Guys who honestly didn't even need to shave as freshmen now looked like they could be grandpas. Some I couldn't even recognize until they told me their names.

But there was Joe Dorsey, looking exactly like he did when he used to throw passes in my direction.

That's when it hit me: I'd known Joe for thirty-nine years—almost four decades! And I made a decision right then that this was a friendship I wanted to keep for life.

After we had talked for a while I asked him, "Hey, what's your e-mail address?"

I love e-mail. It's amazing what it can do to nurture long-distance friendships. Joe and I still can't get together in person on a regular basis, but we know what's going on in each other's life, and it's amazing how quickly the old bond fired itself back up once we started communicating again.

Joe and I used to go to church together, we sang in the choir together, and today we're still seeking to do some of the same things. Joe's working with the church youth group that I grew up with, and I'm pouring my life into kids, singing around the country, and helping to keep Rocketown (a ministry to youth) going. Joe told me he loves hearing kids talk about how one of my songs has encouraged them. We're working toward the same ends.

Ultimately, I believe God plants certain people in our lives. At first, we may not understand why, but in time we will. I've had several relationships, maintained largely through E-mail, that proved their importance when a life crisis came up and the friend needed someone to talk to.

Some friends just fall into our lives—maybe we

live next door, work alongside them, or end up in a small group together. Others, we seem to meet by "divine appointment." A more recent friend of mine, who falls in the later category, is Jeff Fisher, head coach of the Tennessee Titans football team. Deb and I first met Jeff and his wife, Julie, at a restaurant.

What attracted me to Jeff from the start was his genuine interest in others. At first I figured that both of us were way too busy to develop a new friendship. But then our daughters got to be pretty good friends. When Jeff would drop his daughter off at our house to visit, he and I would end up talking. Before we knew it, our friendship had deepened. Now, even though both Jeff and I lead busy lives, we make it a point to get together often.

How do we choose good friends like Joe Dorsey and Jeff Fisher? The Bible offers a lot of wisdom on the subject.

WISDOM'S WORDS

The book of Proverbs was written three thousand years ago, but it still contains some of the best advice ever written on how to choose your friends. The choices we make in this area are crucial. As Stu Weber puts it, "Friends are like highways; they lead somewhere." And Proverbs 12:26 adds this warning: "The righteous should choose his friends carefully, for the way of the wicked leads them astray."

Eventually, the friends we make end up making us. Weber again: "You've seen it in your friends, you've seen it in your kids, you've seen it in yourself. We begin to talk like each other. We tend to adjust to each other. We pick up each other's accents and expressions. We laugh at the same kind of dumb jokes and hum the same tunes. We begin to act like one another, and even dress like each other…

"So, given our propensity to conform, who we hang out with becomes a large factor in our lives. *Who* we hang out with has an incredible influence on *how* we live. *Who* we travel with has a way of determining *where* we end up."[1]

Proverbs 13:20 couldn't be clearer: "He who walks with wise men will be wise, but the companion of fools will be destroyed."

One writer tells the true story of a client of his, a God-fearing young man who signed up to join the military during the Vietnam War. When he left home, he had a bright future. He was a good student, a hard worker, and a practicing Christian. His parents were very proud of him and everybody expected big things from him. They were surprised that he signed up to go to war, but he thought it was the right thing to do.

When he arrived in Nam, he was desperate for a friend and found one that was less than ideal, to say the least. This guy was renowned for breaking all the rules. He stretched every regulation to the breaking point, and then some. He used drugs, introduced his new friend to the Vietnam brothels, and basically just led the guy astray.

You can't imagine how shocked everybody was in that guy's hometown when he was eventually kicked out of the military and dishonorably discharged—a sick drug addict whose life had become a mess.

"So what happened to him?" everybody wanted to know.

Easy answer. He picked the wrong friend.

Choosing the wrong companions won't necessarily wreck your life overnight, but as the weeks, months, and years pass, you'll be changed. And it won't be for the better. You'll take on your friends' values. You'll do things to please them instead of God. You'll slowly grow cold to the things that used to mean the most to you.

DON'T GO DOWN THAT ROAD

Certain kinds of people don't make good friends. Proverbs warns us to stay away from *those who are ruled by anger:* "Make no friendship with an angry man, and with a furious man do not go, lest you learn his ways and set a snare for your soul" (Prov. 22:24–25).

Proverbs also tells us to avoid *violent* people: "A violent man entices his neighbor, and leads him in a way that is not good" (Prov. 16:29). If you're hanging with a group of folks who are always looking for trouble or are quick to pick a fight, you're hanging with the wrong crowd.

We're further warned about *gossips:* "A perverse man sows strife, and a whisperer separates the best of friends" (Prov. 16:28). If the only thing holding you and someone together is that you both love to talk negatively about others, the friendship is doing you more harm than good.

Some friends are in a relationship only for what they can get out of it. These are the *enterprising* people who might be after our money (Prov. 19:4), our influence, or our generosity (Prov. 19:6). They pretend to be our friends only to get something in return.

I faced this early on in my career. Because I knew Amy Grant and was also a recording artist, I began to sense that people wanted to be my friend for all the wrong reasons. It didn't take me long to learn that some of them just wanted to break into the business. They wouldn't have had anything to do with me if I hadn't been somewhat successful in my career.

Maybe that's why I'm particularly sensitive in this area, especially in my friendship with Jeff Fisher. Because some people have had ulterior motives in their relationships with me, I've bent over backward to guard our friendship. We're friends, not just because he's an NFL coach. If he were to quit tomorrow, I'd still be just as interested in who he is and how he's doing, and he feels the same about me. Even though both of us might be considered "celebrities," that's not what our friendship is about.

In fact, not long ago Jeff dropped by the house. I had just released a new CD, and was working on finishing this book; Jeff's team was preparing to play the Baltimore Ravens in a key play-off game. You know what? We didn't talk football, and we didn't talk about this book or my record. We probably talked about hunting or fishing or how much we love our kids. That's what friendship is all about.

~

Another thing to look out for when choosing friends is flattery. "A man who flatters his neighbor spreads a net for his feet" (Prov. 29:5). A lot of insincere talk goes on in Nashville: "Hey, Michael, your last album was *huge*. We've just *got* to get together and do lunch some time." From their tone of voice, I know they'd never look twice at me if my records started to bomb.

Other people may act friendly, but when we're really down, they won't be willing or able to encourage us. Sometimes, Christians can be the worst at this. When your heart is broken, you don't need a glib "all things work for good." You want a friend who will hurt with you, even cry with you, not someone who doesn't want to deal with your grief.

Finally, watch out for the "friend" who doesn't recognize when humor gets out of hand: "Like a madman who throws firebrands, arrows, and death, is the man who deceives his neighbor, and says, 'I was only joking!'" (Prov. 26:18–19). I think it's great to hang with guys that you have a good time with. All of us probably need to laugh more than we do—but not when that laughter comes at someone else's expense.

THE GOOD ROAD

We've just talked about some friends to avoid. But what does Proverbs have to say about the ones you should seek out? Instead of a friend who flatters, look for someone who will be *honest:* "Faithful are the wounds of a friend, but the kisses of an enemy are deceitful" (Prov. 27:6).

I have a couple of guys in my life who tell me the truth, regardless of how they think I'll handle it. Two that come to mind are Don Finto (you've met him in this book before) and Michael Guido. If Don and Mike think I'm straying at all, they're in my face: "What's going on, Michael? Are you covered in accountability? Are you sure you need to do that?"

One of the things I appreciate about some of the guys in our church prayer group is that they're not afraid of constructive confrontation. I need that. Since I'm my own boss and really don't have to answer to anybody vocationally, I need someone to call me to account from time to time. After somebody from that group disagrees with me, I don't get angry. Instead, I think, *You know what? That was really healthy. I'm so thankful I have people who are bold enough to speak challenge into my life.*

If you try to be the kind of person who speaks honestly rather than one who flatters, don't expect to be immediately rewarded. In fact, at first your friend may resent what you have to say. But if what you said is true, and it's said in love, eventually he or she will see that: "He who rebukes a man will find more favor afterward than he who flatters with the tongue" (Prov. 28:23).

We're also told to seek (and to be) *loyal* friends: "Do not forsake your own friend or your father's friend" (Prov. 27:10). I know a woman who, as a teenager, made a pact with her best friend. They agreed that, no matter what, they would *always* tell each other the truth and never gossip about the other. They wanted to avoid the type of talking that splits up friendships real fast. I think that kind of pact is a good idea.

Another good quality to look for in a friend is wisdom—someone who can counsel us. "Ointment and perfume delight the heart, and the sweetness of a man's friend gives delight by hearty counsel" (Prov. 27:9). Advice needs to be tactful, though. A good friend knows not only *what* to say, but *how* to say it, and *when*: "He who blesses his friend with a loud voice, rising early in the morning, it will be counted a curse to him" (Prov. 27:14).

Proverbs also warns that good friends don't always agree with each other. Sometimes, you end up butting heads, but that's part of what being a friend is all about: "As iron sharpens iron, so a man sharpens the countenance of his friend" (Prov. 27:17).

I think it's also important to find friends you can have a good time with. Ecclesiastes 3:4 says there's "a time to weep, and a time to laugh." The psalmist adds, "Then our mouth was filled with laughter, and our tongue with singing" (Ps. 126:2). When I think of some of the best times of my life, I think of Mike Blanton. I have the greatest memories with Mike—dreaming about the future, recording in London with the London Symphony, playing golf in Colorado. Mike and I are more alike than anybody I know, and it's a kick to have a friend like that. We have so much in common that some people have wondered if we were brothers. He does far more than make me laugh, though; he's incredibly inspirational, and I believe his greatest gift is the gift of encouragement. If you spend thirty minutes with Mike, you feel like you could conquer the world.

Another thing I like about Mike is how he spurs me on in my walk with God. The reason I got involved with Mike Blanton and Dan Harrell's company is that they had tremendous vision; they didn't think anything was out of reach. They weren't cocky, just confident. I was so impressed with that. We dreamed big, and a lot of those dreams have come true. I've walked with them through nineteen years and fourteen albums, and not once did they lose sight of the real purpose. Both men would ask me, "Michael, where's your heart at? How's your walk with God?" A really good friend is someone who is spiritually mature and who helps build your faith. Abraham Kuyper (1837–1920), a writer, minister, and former Dutch prime minister, wrote, "He is your friend who pushes you nearer to God."[2]

That's the type of friend the apostle Paul was. Writer James Houston comments, "The key feature of Paul's prayer life is that it dominates all his relationships with other people. His style of writing is saturated with the spirit of prayer in all its forms: pouring out love to God, asking God, giving thanks, praising God for His goodness. His greetings, his farewells, his travel plans, his tellings-off, his hopes and concerns, his communication of the truth—all are cast in the mold of a man who was jealous that the glory of God should become obvious in the lives of his converts."[3]

For the purpose of this book, I'd like to change Houston's comments just a bit to read: We should seek friends who are eager for the glory of God to become obvious in our lives.

Don Finto is one friend who is really eager for God's glory to be evident in my life. I'll never forget something he said to me in the eighties. Things were going pretty well for me professionally in that decade. That's when I began playing to sell-out arenas. It was a very exciting time for me, and I can still remember walking back to my dressing room after the show with tears in my eyes, thinking, *How did I ever get here?*

One of the reasons I was able to keep my head on my shoulders is something Don said to me in Seattle in the late eighties, during the Big Picture Tour. We played in the old hockey arena, built for the world's fair. It was Halloween night and everybody was pumped. Seattle has always been a great market. We played the show and as we walked off the stage, people started pounding their feet with thunderous applause, wanting an encore.

This is unbelievable, I thought. When I stepped behind the curtain, I heard three girls calling out my name. "We love you, Michael! We love you!" It was so strange, I didn't really know what to do, so I just waved, which made them scream even more.

I have to confess, I started thinking, *This is pretty cool for a runt from West Virginia.*

At exactly that moment, I felt a little tap on my shoulder. I turned and saw Don. "It's not you," he said. "It's not you. Give it up, Michael. Give it up."

I'll never forget that moment. Don was right. That experience helped prepare me for the next stage in my career. Now, when the applause gets huge, I can still hear Finto's words, "It's not you. Give it up, Michael. Give it up." All of us need to find friends like Don Finto, friends who help us press into the heart of God. It's a neccessity of life. You've got to plug in somewhere—church, Young Life, youth group. More than likely, that's where you'll find friends for a lifetime.

THE NIGHT I ALMOST DIED

What does all this mean? We need to choose our friends carefully, because the relationships we spend time in are ultimately reflected in our own face and character. We become like the people we hang out with. Choosing the wrong friends can literally kill us. I know, because one night, I almost died.

At the end of my junior year in high school, I hung out with some great kids. I was sort of a Jesus freak, attending Bible studies five times a week, but I was also the youngest in the group. As they went off to college or got married, the group dwindled. So did my spiritual passion. Feeling quite alone, and looking for a place to go, I started spending time with other kids. I knew I was playing with fire by hanging out with some of these guys. They were definitely from the wrong crowd—the partying kind—but I thought I could stick around them without getting burned myself.

One guy was into music; that was our common thread. So we started playing together and I got lured into the party lifestyle, even smoking pot. At first I felt guilty, but after a while my conscience didn't bother me anymore. It was deception all the way, and it almost took me down.

When I arrived in Nashville, I was really deceived. I started playing with an after-hours band at a Holiday Inn. After the last night of our run, we went to someone's house and started snorting cocaine. As the youngest guy in the band and eager for acceptance, I joined in.

In one room, I saw a big mirror with a huge white line of powder running down it. I took up a hundred-dollar bill and snorted up half of it, thinking it was cocaine—but it was THC, a strong tranquilizer. People smoke THC, they don't snort it, but if someone does snort it, it's incredibly dangerous to do very much because it's awfully potent stuff.

Almost immediately, my eyes rolled up into my head, the blood vessels broke in my nose, and I started bleeding all over the place. Some of my friends took me into the bathroom to try to clean me up; my head was spinning like crazy.

I kept thinking, *I'm gonna die. This is it. I'm gonna die.* I couldn't talk—my speech was way too slurry—but I could pray. So I begged God to keep me alive.

Today I think back on that terrible night and wonder, *How in the world did I ever get into that situation?* It just blows my mind that I could be so stupid. The truth is, I didn't really want to go to that party;

I just wanted to fit in. But I got deceived—and it almost cost me my life.

Please learn from my stupidity. Don't get involved with the wrong crowd. Find people like Mike Blanton and Don Finto. If you don't have that kind of support, Satan will take you down.

I can't say it any straighter than this: The friends you choose will make a huge difference in your life. *Those choices better be good ones!*

CHAPTER FOUR

I Will Be
Your Friend

*J*ust how important is it to our own health to learn how to be a good friend to others? Dr. Alan Loy McGinnis, a seasoned counselor, says, "In research at our clinic, my colleagues and I have discovered that friendship is the springboard to every other love."[1] Maybe that's what Jesus was talking about when He told His disciples, "No longer do I call you servants . . . but I have called you friends" (John 15:15). Jesus could have just made us like robots. With forceful threats of hell, He could have simply terrorized His disciples into obedience. But Jesus wasn't after "loyal subjects." He wasn't interested in mere servants, either.

He wanted friends.

Maybe that's why so many millions of people have been so devoted to Jesus Christ for thousands of years. Napoleon said it best: "Alexander [the Great], Caesar, and Hannibal conquered the world but had no friends . . . Jesus founded His empire upon love, and at this hour millions would die for Him . . . He has won the hearts of men, a task a conqueror cannot do."

In his excellent book, *The Friendship Factor,* McGinnis gives five "rules" for deepening your friendships.[2]

Make Friendship a Priority

The first rule McGinnis lists is to "assign top priority to your relationships." McGinnis is talking about deeply meaningful relationships here, not mere acquaintances. "Getting close to a few people is more important than being popular enough to receive 400 Christmas cards every year."[3] It's a matter of choice. Are you willing to invest the time necessary to really get to know someone?

This type of friendship doesn't "just happen." You have to *make* it happen. Most of us are busy enough that if friendship is left to chance, it will never be planted, much less bloom. If our hectic schedules leave no time for our friendships, we'll eventually lose some very important relationships. Samuel Johnson once wrote, "If a man does not make new acquaintances through life, he will soon find himself left alone. A man, Sir, should keep his friendships in constant repair."[4]

That's why, in spite of a pretty busy schedule, I still make time to keep solid friendships going strong. I've already mentioned using e-mail to do this, but I also try to tie friends into things I enjoy doing. In fact, a nurturing friendship is one of the biggest fringe benefits of golf—playing eighteen holes with someone provides a chance to catch up and find out what's really going on in his life.

Now, I'll be honest: When you've got a family, you're not going to have twenty really deep friendships. I don't think it's possible to have that many close relationships, at least not if you're going to give your family the time they need and deserve. At this point in my life, I have what I would characterize as "a deep relationship" with just a few people, though I have a lot of friends.

The best kind of friendship is one in which a month might pass without seeing or talking to each other. But as soon as you get on the phone together, you pick up right where you left off. There's no awkwardness or jealousy about how long it's been since you're talked; instead, you're both just totally focused on being there for each other.

Friendships are so incredibly important. We can't reach the world without them. To be honest, I do wish there was more time in my life for even more friendships than I have—and there probably will be when my kids move out. But I'm still committed to keeping the friendships I have going strong. Friendships are a top priority for me.

Be Real

The second rule McGinnis offers to help build healthy friendships is to "cultivate transparency." This

isn't as easy as it seems. Most of us have some con-
tradictory feelings swirling around inside us; we *want*
to be known, but we're *scared* of being known at the
same time. *If they really know me*, we ask ourselves,
will they still like me? McGinnis explains, "We vacillate
between the impulse to reveal ourselves and the
impulse to protect ourselves with a blanket of privacy.
We long both to be known and to remain hidden."

One of the reasons we have a hard time opening up is because we've been hurt in the past. I
grew up in a small town; if you shared a secret, the
next day a hundred people would know all about it.
I remember telling a group of my guy friends
about some feelings I had for a girl. "Hey guys," I
said, "let's just keep this between us, okay?"

They all agreed, but by lunchtime the next day,
everybody in the school knew how I felt. That
might seem like such a small thing, but you know
what? Even today—twenty-five years later—I can
still feel the hurt and the feelings of betrayal that I
struggled with after realizing I had entrusted something to my closest friends and they had used it to
hurt me. That kind of thing makes it hard to open
up again to others.

One other time I fell really hard for a girl in West Virginia, just before I moved south to Nashville. We were great friends, and then we started dating. She was so much fun that I fell pretty deeply in love, the biggest crush I'd ever had up to that point in my life. As far as I was concerned, things couldn't have been any better, until one day she said, "Michael, I feel like I need to see other people. I don't want to tie myself down right now."

Even though she was nice about it, her words nearly destroyed me. I had never been hurt so badly, and it took me years to trust anybody again. It's hard to explain, but I really thought she liked me—and then she dropped the big bomb! The hurt went so deep that, several years later, I waited almost six months before signing my first recording contract. It was actually that difficult for me to trust. I should have been falling all over myself in eagerness to sign that contract—it was the dream of a lifetime—but once someone has disappointed you, you don't just "get over it"; it takes time.

I think another reason some people refuse to open up is that they fear being rejected, but McGinnis says that such a fear is usually misguided.

"As I have watched patients in all kinds of . . . situations, I have found that self-disclosure has the opposite effect. When people take off their masks, others are drawn to them."[5]

I think that's true; at least, it has been for me. My closest friends are the ones I know the best—the ones who have been the most honest. When I know somebody isn't being genuine, the friendship won't go very far. I grew up with a guy and started to build a fairly decent friendship with him, but after a while, things weren't adding up; he would say one thing, but do something else. A couple of times I caught him telling me something that didn't sound true. But when he offered an explanation, I always gave him the benefit of the doubt—until it became obvious that this just wasn't a guy I could trust, which also meant he wasn't the type of guy I could build a deep friendship with.

Such shallowness happens all the time in Nashville. I love living here, but to be perfectly honest, Nashville has enough ambition for a medium-sized country, let alone a city. A lot of people come here with a big dreams, and they'll use you to get what they want if they think you can help them.

I used to work with a guy that I really liked. We got along great, and I was impressed by his credentials. He said he had been a star quarterback for his team, had an impressive college degree, and we seemed to click really well—until I found out that nothing he had told me was true. The degree was a fake, and he hadn't even been on the football team, much less starred as quarterback.

Another mutual friend finally blew this guy's cover: "Look, Michael," he said, "I'm not trying to spread rumors or talk behind someone's back, but you need to know what's going on. I'm worried about how this guy might be trying to use you." When I talked to the guy directly, he admitted that he'd made up most of what he'd been bragging about.

Even with stories like these in my past, it's still not that hard for me to be transparent now, but I am careful about it. I don't open up to just anybody, and I'm not completely transparent the first or second time I get together with somebody. If I don't feel like I can trust someone, I don't feel obligated to open up to him or her.

But all of us need to learn how to be open and

real with a few close friends. McGinnis goes so far as to suggest, "You can never genuinely know yourself except as an outcome of disclosing yourself to another. When you reveal yourself to another person, you learn how to increase contact with your real self."[6] In other words, when you aren't honest with somebody, you're probably not being honest with yourself, either. You're actually hiding from yourself.

When people have a problem with lying, their life story usually reveals some pretty scary stuff that's happened in their past, frequently involving their home life: a parent was abusive, or they didn't find the security and love they needed when they were growing up, so they learned to relate by lying and manipulation instead of honesty. If that's the case, this person needs to go to a counselor and get the truth out in the open before learning how to be a good friend.

Speak Your Heart

McGinnis's third step is, "Dare to talk about your affection." He mentions an awards ceremony where Gale Sayers, one of the best running backs in all of NFL history, had the guts to say: "You flatter me by giving me this award, but I tell you here and now that I accept it for Brian Piccolo. Brian Piccolo [who was in the hospital fighting cancer at the time] is the man of courage who should receive the George S. Halas Award. I love Brian Piccolo and I'd like you to love him."

Jesus was quick to tell people how much He thought of them. When a despicable centurion trusted in Jesus, He said, loud enough for everyone to hear, "Assuredly, I say to you, I have not found such great faith, not even in Israel!" (Matt. 8:10) What Jesus did here is pretty radical. Today, it would be like showing up at a Baptist or Presbyterian church, picking out an obvious sinner of some type (fill in the blank for yourself) who had never set foot in a church before, and telling everyone, "This person has more faith than anyone else in this room!"

Jesus told an entire city, "O Jerusalem, Jerusalem . . . How often I wanted to gather your children together, as a hen gathers her chicks under her wings, but you were not willing!" (Matt. 23:37). There is no fear in Jesus' mind about sounding "mushy." When He loved or admired someone, He said so.

Jesus' speech was filled with terms of endearment: "Son, be of good cheer" (Matt. 9:2), and "Be of good cheer, daughter" (Matt. 9:22). Even when Jesus enlisted people to do His work, He made sure they knew how passionately God felt about them, telling them that He had counted every hair on their heads (Matt. 10:30).

If Jesus didn't have a problem with sentimental musings, then why do we? I think this area is more difficult for guys than women. Sometimes it's hard for a guy to tell another guy, "I really care about you." When we grow up, we want to be the "tough guy"; never cry, always be strong, don't let 'em see you sweat. Well, who says a man shouldn't cry or tell another man that he really cares about him?

When I was younger, it was much more difficult for me to express my feelings. It even took me a while to tell my dad I loved him. I got past that when I realized, *What if I never see my dad again?* I knew I would regret for the rest of my life, not telling him how I felt. Since that time, I think I've been making up for it; I tell my dad I love him all the time now.

McGinnis tells how Thomas Jefferson—a "man's man"—maintained close relationships with other guys without embarrassment. He wrote to John Adams, "Take care of your health and be assured that you are most dear to me." When he finally got to see his good friend and war hero Lafayette, whom he hadn't seen in thirty-five years but with whom he had corresponded on a regular basis, the two men collapsed into each other's arms, tears flowing down their cheeks.

Are you willing to open up and tell your friends just how important they are to you, and how much they mean to you? You don't want to pressure them with this, or use it with expectation—saying how much you care about them only to hear it back— but it's important that we tell people how we really feel about them.

Learn to Love

Friendship doesn't come automatically to any of us. We're all born selfish, and adolescence is a time in life when it's standard practice to be self-absorbed. Katherine Anne Porter wrote, "Love must be learned, and learned again and again; there is no end to it. Hate needs no instruction, but waits only to be provoked."[8]

Learning the art of friendship, then, means learning what it means to love. I'm using love as a verb here, not as a feeling. It's the little things that build a friendship—a note of encouragement, a phone call, remembering a birthday, an unexpected gift, being there when someone is down. That's why McGinnis's fourth rule for building friendships is, "Learn the gestures of love."

As I've already mentioned, I've known the Titans coach for a couple of years now. One day I had watched a particularly close game that Tennessee really should have won but lost on a field goal just as time expired. I knew Jeff would be upset, so I called him up and left a message on his voice mail, saying something like, "Just wanted to let you know that I love you, Jeff. I believe God put us together as friends for a reason. You could be 0–16, and it wouldn't affect our relationship. Just wanted you to know that."

To me, that's what being a friend is all about. You're there for the tough times as well as the good times. You don't have to be royalty to be a friend. You don't have to be a movie star, a great athlete, a supermodel, or an NFL quarterback. What you *do* need is to learn how to love, how to be kind. No less brilliant a man than Leonardo da Vinci said, "The ministry of kindness is a treasured aspect of friendship which may be inherited by all men, rich and poor, learned and illiterate. Brilliance of mind and capacity for deep thinking have rendered great service to humanity, but by themselves they are impotent to dry a tear or mend a broken heart."[9]

Jeff doesn't how rich I am, how smart I am, or how many records I've sold. He wants somebody to share his frustrating times. That's what we all want, isn't it? Walter Winchell once said, "A real friend is one who walks in when the rest of the world walks out."[10]

If you really want to learn the art of friendship, learn how to do little acts of kindness. Go out of your way to show you care. I think I've finally discovered that it's not about me; it's about standing in the gap for other people.

Create Space

McGinnis warns, "One personality trait gets the prize for ruining more relationships than any other. It is a characteristic found to some degree in each of us, but when it gets out of hand, it is always destructive and always pushes people away.

"I am talking about the tendency to control others."[11]

Friendship requires freedom, so McGinnis gives as his fifth principle, "Create space in your relationships." If you want to be a good friend, make sure you're not becoming a controlling friend. Ask yourself, "Do I always insist that we do what I want to do? That we see the movies I want to see and eat at the restaurants where I want to eat?" Or, on the other hand, do you suffocate someone by being overly weak, always asking for their help, always needing their attention, and acting jealous if they build any other friendships?

I once had a friend who called *all the time*. He was nice enough about it: "How you doing, Michael? Everything okay? Just checking in. Wanted to hook up." His calls could be that basic, but the sheer volume of them really started to feel unhealthy, like I was becoming a security blanket for him. Over time, they became very draining, threatening our relationship. Consequently, we don't talk that much anymore.

Don't get me wrong: he was a wonderful guy and a good friend at that point in my life, but he just didn't know when to stop. Remember the proverb: "Seldom set foot in your neighbor's house, lest he become weary of you" (Prov. 25:17).

Other friends might "crowd" us by wanting to get more "intense." Do you have any friends like this? They always want to go "deeper," whether it's personal sharing or theological discussions. It's not that I'm in favor of "shallow" relationships, but sometimes you detect that someone has almost an unhealthy desire to go deeper.

In some cases, these people just need to find another type of friend. One woman calls me and wants to get into these heavy theological conversations, but that's not my expertise. I'm pretty much a black-and-white kind of guy; I see things for the way they are, and try to apply Scripture as best I can. I'm not the kind of friend you want if you're looking for someone who will debate the most obscure theological points long into the night. That's just not me. She needs to find a seminary professor!

I've had my own struggles with giving friends space. When I first moved to Nashville, I started regularly calling a friend of mine in the music business. He was helping me to break into the business, and is one of the main reasons I got my chance. I was so excited about all that was happening that I started calling him at all hours of the day.

Somewhere along the way, I crossed a line. I remember calling him once when he said, "Michael, you've got to stop calling me at home. I'm not trying to hurt your feelings, but we need to talk when I'm at the office, not when I'm home with my family."

When I hung up, my feelings *were* hurt, but the more I thought about it, the more I realized he was right; I had been acting like a leech. Obviously, there was some kind of a void in my life that I was trying to use him to fill, and it was unhealthy and unfair.

We've all probably had periods where we wanted a closer friendship with someone than that person felt comfortable with. McGinnis explains, "Clutching behavior comes from overworking and overloading one relationship. The antidote for jealousy is to expand your own interests and to make friends in several groupings. No one person is ever going to 'make you happy.' Your life must encompass multiple interests, passions in many areas, and several relationships if you are to avoid crowding any of your loved ones."[12]

So then, if you want to improve the friendships you already have, McGinnis advises these five things: make friendship a priority, learn to be more transparent, speak your heart, learn to love and focus on the other guy, and—while you do all the above—don't forget to create space and leave the other person room to breathe.

That's a pretty good recipe for life.

CHAPTER FIVE

Friendship Follies

ne of the longest nights of my life happened during a particularly snowy winter in West Virginia. Jimmy Bloss picked me up in one of his father's cars. His dad was a car dealer, so Jimmy always had his pick of vehicles. Tonight it was an AMC Ambassador.

"Hey, Mike," he said, "let's go out to Virginia Point."

Virginia Point is a boat dock of sorts, a popular party place within sight of three state borders: Kentucky, Ohio, and West Virginia. Kids always went down there to hang out and party. It was a late Sunday evening and really starting to snow.

"No, I don't want to go down there," I told Jimmy. "I'm afraid we'll get stuck."

"Come on, Mike. It'll be great. We can do doughnuts in the snow."

Jimmy kept pressing so I finally gave in. By now the snow was falling harder and harder, and I was getting nervous, but Jimmy was determined. We slid down a small hill as we neared the boat ramp—completely deserted, as nobody else was foolish enough to go out there on a night like this—and quickly realized the snow was too deep for doughnuts Instead, Jimmy turned the car around and prepared to gun it as fast as he could to see if we could make it back up the snowy hill.

We made it halfway up.

That car wasn't going anywhere. It fishtailed off the road and sank into the snow. It's one thing to be stuck in the snow; it's another thing altogether to be stuck in the snow when you're out in the middle of nowhere.

We got out of the car and started walking. It was bitterly cold, but at least I wasn't wearing the six-inch platform shoes Jimmy had on. (In the seventies, those big-heeled shoes were considered "far out" for guys.)

When you're young and without money, your first thought is, *How do I get out of this mess without having to pay anything?* We walked to a restaurant called the Midget Carry-Out to phone some friends, but nobody could make it out there to help us.

"My dad has a wrecking service he always uses," Jimmy finally said. "I'm sure they'll send a wrecker over to pull us out."

He was a little overconfident. When the dispatcher found out where we were, he turned us down. "Boys, with this much snow, this is the busiest night of the year. There's no way I'm going to send a truck all the way down there to get one car. I'd lose too much money. I'm sorry, but you're just gonna have to wait."

Jimmy played politics, reminding the dispatcher

of how much service he got from his dad's car dealership. Finally, the guy relented and said he'd send a truck to pull us out.

We walked back to the car and waited. The snow was still falling, a foot deep by now. When we saw the wrecker our hearts lifted—until the guy started sliding down the hill . . . and into the ditch! I won't repeat what the driver said when he ordered a second wrecker to come get *him* out.

The second wrecker barely crested the hill when it got stuck too. Now the dispatcher was really ticked—not only had they lost the services of one wrecker on the busiest night of the year, they had lost *two!*

This was getting beyond ridiculous; it was flat-out ugly.

Jimmy and I started trying to dig out by ourselves, without much success. When the police department sent a car over to check on things, I jumped into their backseat to warm up. It was then I noticed Jimmy laughing. "What's up?" I yelled out the window.

He pointed to the rear tire. When I looked, I saw that it was flat. The police officer sighed, then got out the jack and spare tire and went to work.

What else could go wrong?

Finally, at about three o'clock in the morning, our friend Lang Chandler showed up with a super jeep of some sort. After about an hour of pulling, he had us out and up the hill, and we were on our way. For the record, the wreckers didn't get out until about 10:00 A.M. the next morning.

When you're with friends, a lot of crazy stuff can happen. Sometimes, these frustrating events can tear friends apart. Other times, it draws you together. Jimmy and I got through it okay—he ended up as a groomsman in my wedding.

I hope you're never stuck on a hill in a snowstorm with any of your friends. Here are a few other things to avoid.

Taking Every Rejection Personally

In their book, *Friends and Friendship,* Terry and Nancy White tell a story that probably repeats itself on virtually every college campus every year:

Allison entered a Christian college, enthusiastic about her studies, activities, and new friendships. Unknown to her, her assigned roommate was attending because her father would finance her studies only at a Christian school and not the state university, which was her first choice.

Allison first met Kate on a hot September afternoon when they were both tired from the drive to the school and both dreading hauling their belongings to the fourth floor of the dormitory.

"Hi," Allison said cheerfully as she entered the room and found Kate sitting on a suitcase. "I'm Allison."

"Yeah? Well, I'm Kate and this sure is a ratty little room and I don't know where I'm going to put all of my things, much less your stuff!"

Over the next several weeks Allison made several attempts to relieve the strained situation and generate a friendship with her roommate, but she was always met with a cutting reply and hostile looks. Finally Allison gave up, and the standoff lasted until the end of the school year.

Allison made other friends on campus, but the constant air of rejection and tension made her wary of opening herself to others. Although she was assigned a congenial roommate the following year, it wasn't until her senior year that she fully came out of the shell her freshman year experience had crowded her into.

Rejection may take time to heal. Unless we decide to overlook a few incidents of rejection throughout our lifetime, we will deny ourselves the delight of many possible friendships.[1]

I know a man who headed a major Christian ministry. His responsibilities required him to be on the road for long stretches of time. A man at his church kept trying to initiate a friendship, but the leader finally pulled him aside and said, "Look, I'd like to be your friend. You seem like someone I could really get along with well. But I'm on the road so much that when I'm home, I need to spend that time with my wife and four daughters. Until they leave home, I really don't have much time to spend with you."

His remarks weren't anything personal—given different circumstances, he probably would have loved getting to know this guy better. But his life situation at the time honestly didn't have room for a new friendship.

There could be any number of reasons someone rejects you, and most of them probably have nothing at all to do with you. Don't assume there's something wrong with you when someone doesn't share your interest in building a relationship; you may just have caught that person at a particularly busy time. Find somebody else and move on.

Intolerance and Prejudice

Jesus was always "accused" of hanging out with "tax collectors and sinners" (Matt. 11:19; Luke 7:34). What a great accusation! Jesus *was* a friend to sinners, and we should be too. The Whites write, "In the life of a Christian, genuine tolerance combined with the love of Jesus Christ will open a wide range of friendship possibilities. It will allow you to cross racial lines, social barriers, age differences, and physical limitations. You will accept personality quirks and failings. A tolerant Christian sees every individual through God's viewpoint—as worthwhile and valuable."[2]

There's a certain type of person who is always going to have a difficult time making and keeping friends: the *arguer*, who uses his intellect like a sword and who has an opinion about everything. I think Abraham Lincoln said it best: "The more arguments you win, the fewer friends you will have."[3]

I'm not suggesting we shouldn't have strong opinions or be willing to occasionally disagree with others, but there's a gentle, wise, and discerning way to do that. Jason Noe, the former Rocketown Director of Ministry, remembers a time when he was in downtown Memphis with a few friends. As they headed down Beale Street, they heard an angry barking, and picked up their pace to see what was going on. Turns out it was a street preacher. Jason said, "He claimed to be spreading the gospel, but all I heard were condemning words of hatred and anger. There was nothing good in what he was saying. There was no love. No compassion. No Jesus."

Then Jason noticed another man on the corner, this one cursing and yelling out that the preacher didn't know what he was talking about. One of Jason's friends, Shawn (who now heads up the Rocketown ministry), went over to talk to the young guy who was cursing. This guy's name was Joey, and Joey explained to Shawn that he had tried to ask the preacher an honest question, but was ignored and then finally rebuked—loudly and blatantly—for being drunk.

Shawn asked Joey if he believed in God, and Joey said yes, he had gone to church as a little boy, but didn't anymore.

"Can I pray for you?" Shawn asked.

Joey's eyes filled with tears. "Yes."

As soon as Shawn said *"Amen,"* Joey grabbed him, hugged him, and said, *"Thank you!"*

Neither Shawn nor the street preacher agreed with Joey's lifestyle—but one of them found a way to talk to Joey; the other just turned Joey off.

What kind of friend do you want to be?

Being Insensitive

I had a friend who had a tendency to "snap." One minute he was a happy-go-lucky kind of guy, very friendly and nice, but the next minute he would suddenly become aggressive and belligerent. It could be intimidating, because there was no way to know when he might go off.

One time we were talking in a public setting. I was careful to keep my voice down so nobody could hear us, but finally he yelled out, "Would you just *shut up? Just shut up!*" It was embarrassing. Other people started looking our way, wondering what was going on.

In the past, when this friend had acted this way, I had wimped out. But this time he really put me over the edge. I don't get mad often, but I was fed up with this guy's sudden explosions.

"You owe me an apology," I said.

"No, I don't," he replied.

"Yes, you do."

"No, I don't."

I wasn't going to sit there and argue with him, so I turned my back and left. I had never done anything like that before, so it really threw him. But I knew if I didn't stand up to him, he'd repeat this behavior with everybody he met for the rest of his life, and it would destroy his relationships.

Twenty minutes later, he came back to my dressing room and said, "You know what? You're right, and I'm sorry."

"I appreciate that," I said, "and I'm sorry too."

This friend hasn't been rude to me since.

We don't often think of insensitivity as a "sin," but it can hurt. If you're always laughing at someone else's expense, if you put others down to make yourself feel better and trying to pass it off as "just good fun," you're not being a true friend. A true friend not only watches what he says; he watches *how* he says says.

Jealousy

You can't really talk about friendship without talking about *jealousy*. Though I'm not the jealous type, there was a time in my life when I struggled with this sin, particularly when I was growing up. You see one of your good friends, maybe even your best friend, start to spend more and more time with someone else—which means they spend less time with you—and you start to feel betrayed. The friendship doesn't feel the same, and you wonder what happened.

Now I feel secure enough that this type of thing is almost never a problem, and the friends I'm closest with feel the same way. Don Finto is delighted that I spend time with Billy Graham. I don't even keep track of how much time one friend spends with another.

I've also gotten over some other jealousy issues.

Back in high school, it could be tough if a close friend went out for the same position in football, or made the basketball team and I didn't. Now I'm in a business that publishes weekly album sales—you can tell exactly how many records you've sold compared to all your friends in the business (which is one reason I have a lot of friends who aren't in the music business).

To be honest, I care less about that stuff today than I ever have in my whole life. I'm delighted when a friend sells a lot of albums, or when other friends of mine, like Sixpence None the Richer, has a huge breakout mainstream hit such as "Kiss Me" or "There She Goes."

Believe it or not, it's even possible to get jealous about ministry! Remember when the disciples caught others casting out demons in Jesus' name? You'd think they'd have been excited that they weren't alone, that there were other groups working for the same cause. You'd think so—but you'd be wrong. Instead, they complained to Jesus: "Master, we saw someone casting out demons in Your name, and we forbade him because he does not follow with us" (Luke 9:49).

Jesus responded, "Do not forbid him, for he who is not against us is on our side" (v. 50).

Friendship is a lot more fun when we can rejoice over someone's success instead of feeling bad about it. We should be happy when God blesses someone with a new house—without comparing that house to our own. We should celebrate a friend's new job—even if we hate ours. We should learn how to genuinely be glad for other people—and when we do that, we increase our own joy!

Jealousy, on the other hand, does nothing but cause bitterness; it fills you full of resentment and anger. One thing I've learned: If you're jealous, you think it's all about you. But it's not about you—it's about learning to care for others. Jealousy mixes up our priorities.

Whenever jealousy comes into play, there's usually a deeper problem somewhere. The jealous person might have some insecurities or might be dealing with some baggage from the past and now is looking for some sort of acceptance. People who are stable in the spiritual realm don't deal with a lot of jealousy, so if you catch yourself falling into this trap, you might want to talk to a pastor or a trusted counselor.

Too Many Demands

Has anyone ever pretended to be your friend—and you later discovered they didn't want to be friends at all? Maybe you've been asked to dinner, only to find that your host was pitching a multi-level marketing plan. At work, someone seemed to take a real interest in you—invited you to lunch and coffee breaks, stopped by your office to see how things were going—until your realized that he was just climbing the corporate ladder and you were the next rung. When a relationship is marked more by the demands made than by the love offered, it's not called friendship, it's called manipulation.

This happens to me sometimes. It seems I've got a relationship going with a good friend when all of a sudden, I hear something like, "Hey, Michael, we've got this event coming up. It's for a great cause, and we'd really like you to appear." I thought this person wanted to be my friend; as it turns out, I'm just being manipulated.

My true friends, the ones I'm closest to, don't put any demands on me at all. That doesn't mean they don't ever ask for anything, but it's the motive behind the request that seems so different. Franklin Graham once asked me to play at six crusades. When I checked my calendar, I saw I couldn't make but three of them.

Franklin didn't blink an eye. "I'll take you when you can come, Michael. In fact, I really appreciate your trying to fit us in at all."

When I did show up, he was genuinely thankful: "Michael, thank you so much for coming. I can't believe you'd even consider it."

Was he kidding? Who wouldn't want to help out with a ministry that reaches to so many people with the Gospel? But with that kind of attitude, you don't feel used; you feel *blessed*.

An Idealized View of Friendship

Have you ever seen someone miss out on a lot of good relationships because they have this ideal picture of what a "best friend" should be? Dietrich Bonhoeffer writes about this in his book *Life Together*. Bonhoeffer made friends in a tough environment—he ran an essentially "illegal" seminary during the Hitler regime. (Dietrich was ultimately killed for his work resisting the German dictator.) People came to the seminary with high ideals and a lot of dreams. They "imagined" what they thought such an experience would be like, and the real experience often fell far short of their fantasies.

"A Christian . . . is likely to bring with him a very definite idea of what Christian life together should be and to try to realize it," Bonhoeffer wrote. "But God's grace speedily shatters such dreams . . .

"Every human wish dream that is injected into the Christian community is a hindrance to genuine community and must be banished if genuine community is to survive. He who loves his dream of a community more than the Christian community itself becomes a destroyer [of that community], even though his personal intentions may be ever so honest and earnest and sacrificial."[4]

Dietrich is talking about Christians who like the *idea* of friendship, but who give up when friendship becomes real—and difficult. They want a best friend, but they get all huffy when that best friend hurts them or ignores them or builds a deep friendship with somebody else. They want friendship on their terms, in their way, under their conditions.

That type of friendship won't work. Two people bring their own dreams into any relationship, but for that relationship to make it, both people have to learn how to compromise. *Real* people may disagree with you, might argue with you, will have their own hopes and expectations.

Don't lose a good friendship because you're intent on finding some ideal that doesn't really exist. Learn to love your friends for who they are, as they are.

"That sounds great, Michael," some of you might be saying. "But how do I *do* that?"

Bonhoeffer has some practical advice. Much of it goes back to how we pray. He counsels us, "We do not complain of what God does not give us; we rather thank God for what He does give us daily."[5] When you pray for your friends, do you spend all your time asking God to change them? "Lord, help Alan to be more sensitive toward me." "God, help Angie to stop being so mean and critical." Or do you thank God for the good things about friendship that you already enjoy: "Lord, thank You for the way I can count on Alan." "God, thank You for the good times I have with Angie."

It's all about focus: we can become obsessed with what friends are *not,* and thereby miss what they really *are.* Remember, other than Jesus, you'll never find a perfect friend.

Gossip

Bonhoeffer had a great rule for his seminary: "Thus it must be a decisive rule of every Christian fellowship that each individual is prohibited from saying much that occurs to him . . . To speak about a brother covertly is forbidden, even under the cloak of help and good will; for it is precisely in this guise that the spirit of hatred among brothers always creeps in when it is seeking to create mischief."[6]

There is an awful lot of Scripture to back up what Bonhoeffer says:

"Do not go about spreading slander among your people" (Lev. 19:16 NIV).

"Do not speak evil of one another, brethren" (James 4:11).

"Let no corrupt word proceed out of your mouth, but what is good for necessary edification, that it may impart grace to the hearers" (Eph. 4:29).

"A perverse man stirs up dissension, and a gossip separates close friends" (Prov. 16:28 NIV).

Gossip destroys the church; it just tears people down, and it's usually based on ignorance. Most people who gossip don't have all the facts, but even if they do, what good is served by passing it on.

I hear gossip all the time. I walk into country clubs or restaurants and see guys playing poker, drinking and smoking, and saying, "Hey, did you hear what Barney got into?" Then there's some lurid story and everybody laughs or cusses or shouts, and I can't help but think, *Don't you have anything better to do with your time?*

Unfortunately, gossip isn't limited to country clubs—it happens in the church and in small towns all across America. Gossip is one of the most destructive sins there is, even though it isn't looked at as seriously as some other evils.

If we quit gossiping, something amazing happens. Bonhoeffer describes it this way:

Where this discipline of the tongue is practiced right from the beginning, each individual will make a matchless discovery. He will be able to cease from constantly scrutinizing the other person, judging him, condemning him, putting him in his particular place where he can gain ascendancy over him and thus doing violence to him as a person. Now he can allow the brother to exist as a completely free person, as God made him to be. His view expands and, to his amazement, for the first time he sees . . . the richness of God's creative glory. God did not make this person as I would have made him. He did not give him to me as a brother for me to dominate and control, but in order that I might find above him the Creator. Now the other person, in the freedom with which he was created, becomes the occasion of joy, whereas before he was only a nuisance and an affliction.[7]

I'm good friends with some well-known people whose marriages didn't make it. Just about every time I was interviewed for a while, people kept asking me for the "inside scoop" on "what really happened."

You know what I think? It's none of my business. Nobody really knows what goes on inside any marriage, except for the two people involved. No purpose is served by talking about it. I hate to see any marriage break up, but God hasn't called me to be anybody's judge—He's called me to be their friend. Sometimes, I do challenge what my friends do—to their face, and in private—but I don't make any of these conversations public. If those couples had wanted my advice, they knew how to reach me. No good could ever come of my talking to a third party about somebody else's private business.

The same thing that's true for me is true for you and your friends: nothing good comes from gossip. There isn't a single marriage that has ever been reconciled due to gossip. Nobody has ever quit using drugs or started drinking less because others gossiped about the situation. No pastor ever became less controlling because people started talking behind his back. Frankly, the only person served by gossip is the devil! When you gossip, you're doing the devil's work on his behalf. It's that simple. Scripture forbids gossip and slander, and we shouldn't have anything to do with it.

Instead of gossiping, I hope we'll take the advice of the great painter Auguste Renoir, who said, "Treat your friends as you do your pictures; place them in their best light."[8]

If you want to build long-lasting friendships, you'll need to avoid these friendship poisons: Don't take rejection personally. Root out intolerance and prejudice. Stay away from insensitivity. Get rid of jealousy. Don't place too many demands on your friends. Watch out for an "idealized" view of friendship that might blind you to the goodness of the friendships you already have. And don't gossip.

You can do everything else right, but if you inject these poisons into a relationship, it's only a matter of time before that relationship dies.

CHAPTER SIX

Two Are Better Than One

hristopher had a big dream. He called it "The Great Enterprise" and spent many a late night plotting the course of the currents, measuring the force of the winds, and documenting the changes in the seasons to see if his huge plans might ever be achieved. Was it really possible to circumnavigate the globe?[1]

Christopher Columbus knew he couldn't complete such an incredible journey on his own, so he approached the king of Portugal, asking for his aid. After eighteen months of deliberations, the king's advisers turned Columbus down. They didn't trust his calculations and thought he was being wildly optimistic in his estimates.

According to George and Karen Grant, "The Portuguese rejection was a stunning blow to Columbus. He was so completely convinced that his plan was the will of God that he had a hard time imagining how or why anyone would question its validity. In his mind it was as preordained as salvation. His confidence was shattered."[2]

Have you ever been in a place like that—convinced that God has called you to do something, but confused that every door seems to be slamming in your face?

Unfortunately for Chris, things got much worse before they got better. Just days after the Portuguese rejected his plans, Columbus's wife died suddenly. In near despair, he packed his belongings and moved with his son to Palos, where he met Fra Antonio de Marchena, a Franciscan friar who also had a reputation for being a top-notch scientist. Columbus and Marchena hit it off right away and became close friends. Soon, Marchena caught Chris's enthusiasm for "The Great Enterprise."

Now Chris was no longer working alone. The Friar helped him refine his plans. He lent Chris new books to increase the young adventurer's reservoir of knowledge. He introduced him to influential people connected with Queen Isabella of Spain. He also made sure that Columbus's son received a first-class education, freeing Columbus up to concentrate on making his dream become a reality.

Columbus got the chance to present his quest to Queen Isabella, who took seven long years to make up her mind, only to turn Columbus down. Christopher was devastated, and nearly broke, so he started to make plans to leave.

Fortunately, his good friend Marchena once again stepped into the fray. Now the head of the friary at La Rabida, Marchena used every political connection and influence he had to make a last-ditch effort on Columbus's behalf. As a result of these efforts, Isabella changed her mind and was joined by her husband, King Ferdinand, in sponsoring Christopher Columbus's historic trip to discover America.

While friends have a high spiritual and emotional value, the right ones can also help us to become all that God meant us to be. Individuals working in isolation rarely achieve great things. The best works usually result from friendships.

Think about it—even Jesus enlisted the help of a few close friends to start the Church. He began by calling twelve disciples, but out of that group, He focused on three—Peter, John, and James.

The friends who help us succeed may not ever be recognized for their assistance—most of you have probably never heard of Marchena, though you've heard of Columbus—but without these quiet friends, history books would be pretty short.

Friendship marks God's method for getting things done. Read Luke 10:1–2, and you'll find that Jesus sent His followers out in pairs. He didn't expect them to face their mission on their own. That's because two people working together can do much more than two people working separately. Stu Weber, the author who is also an avid hunter, explains that a flock of geese, flying in a V formation, increase their flying range by at least 71 percent, as opposed to each bird flying on its own. He also points out that at one county fair, one draft horse was able to pull a sled weighing 4,500 pounds. The second-place horse could drag just 4,000 pounds. Someone suggested putting the two draft horses together. Working as a team, they pulled 12,000 pounds.[3]

The writer of Ecclesiastes expresses this well:

Two are better than one,
Because they have a good reward for their labor.
For if they fall, one will lift up his companion.
But woe to him who is alone when he falls,
For he has no one to help him up. (Eccl. 4:9–10)

It shouldn't be too surprising that the apostle Paul followed Jesus' example and also built some friendships as he worked on God's behalf. Two of his closest friends were Aquila and Priscilla, a married couple who shared Paul's skills as tentmakers. Paul lived with them in Corinth (Acts. 18:2–3). The friendship was fruitful; shortly thereafter, Aquila and Priscilla were teaching others themselves (Acts 18:26), eventually instructing Apollos, a powerful teacher in the first century. Aquila and Priscilla left Corinth with Paul and traveled with him to Ephesus. At one point, they even risked their lives for him (Rom. 16:3–4).

Paul mentions other close friends in his letters: Fortunatus, Achaicus (1 Cor. 16:17), Tychicus (Eph. 6:21), Timothy, Justus, and Epaphras (Col. 4:11–12), and many, many others. In fact, Paul used his friendship with Philemon (whom he calls a "beloved friend" in Philemon 1) to give him leverage in asking for mercy on behalf of the runaway slave Onesimus.

One thing is clear: Paul wasn't a "lone ranger." He worked hard for God on his own, but whenever possible, he worked with others.

WORKING TOGETHER

Friends have played a big role in my own success. I didn't build these relationships *because* they could help me succeed, but after we hooked up, the connections consequently opened a lot of doors. The music business is based on friendships and trust. I'm sure that Amy Grant wouldn't have allowed me to write all those songs with her if I had been a jerk. We hit it off creatively, established a friendship, and both of us have leaned on each other in different periods of our lives.

Here's the key though: I never thought of getting to know Amy as my entryway into the music business. Yes, opening for her shows and writing songs with her played a part in landing my own record deal, but that's not the reason I was her friend. Amy would have seen through that, anyway. But writing songs together did play a part in our friendship. I guess you could say work brought us together, but our love for each other has held us together.

Being friends with those you work with makes work that much more fun. One such friend is Don Donahue. I first met Don on the Big Picture tour. He was a little "wet behind the ears," maybe twenty years old at that time, but he got someone with a little bit of money to put on a concert in Missouri and helped to promote that show. It was fun being around him, but I didn't see him again until three years later, when he came down to Nashville to work for Reunion Records.

Don was an A & R (Artists and Relations) guy. We worked on several albums, not so much on the creative end (though Don was occasionally involved in this side too), but we did spend many a night listening to songs for the next album, becoming pretty good friends in the process. That's why I immediately thought of Don when I considered starting Rocketown Records.

I had dreamed of launching my own label for a long time. From the start, my desire was to create something that felt like family—small, intimate, and artist-focused. I've seen a lot of great talent out there, and always wanted a vehicle to help develop it, but I wanted to do so by taking a whole different approach from that of "corporate" record companies—rather than signing a lot of artists, I wanted to find a few who could gel with us and who would be committed to what we were trying to accomplish.

When I started thinking seriously about forming Rocketown Records, Don was one of the first guys I talked to. We met at my farm and started walking and talking, sharing out loud our dreams

about starting a new label, what would make it different, how we could do things that a corporate
house could not (or would not) do.

After many months of dreaming, we realized
we had the same vision. We were most interested
in artists who wrote their own songs ("If you don't
have a song, you don't have a record," we often
say). We wanted to bring more integrity to the
business, as well as make it more relational. Instead
of just crunching numbers, we wanted to become
mentors to younger artists, helping them develop
as individuals and as artists. We honestly didn't care
if the music was heavy metal or blue grass or
pop—if the musicians were singer/songwriters of
talent and integrity, we wanted to give them a
chance.

We had a "Rocketown Meeting" in 1997 to
launch the label, where we had artist performances
and speakers, but also focus groups that could give
us feedback. We wanted listeners' suggestions,
ideas, and opinions to be taken seriously. It might
sound corny, but we really did want to create a new
"family" of music.

Because Rocketown is based on relationships,

we often make decisions that executives would shy away from. I remember when Chris Rice came in and played for us for the first time. The rage at that time was all the polished acts—DC Talk, Jars of Clay, that sort—and Chris's music was nothing like that. Even so, his depth and talent blew us away, and we knew we had to make him our first artist.

For a while, it didn't make much sense to hire a James Taylor–type singer to launch a label, and both Don and I asked each other, "Have we lost our minds?" But ultimately we decided to trust our gut feelings. "This things gonna work," we kept saying—and we were right. Chris has been phenomenally successful, as we knew he would be.

A bigger company might not have been able to take that chance.

What about your dreams, your work, your ministry? Are you tired of trying to do it all on your own? If you are, remember Jesus' model: Gather some close friends around you and work together. It's much more effective and much more enjoyable when we do God's work—God's way.

CHAPTER SEVEN

Fractured Friendships

*H*ave you ever had a friendship go sour? Maybe it happened slowly. Your best friend stopped calling as frequently, and you couldn't help noticing that something had changed. When you brought it up—"Is something wrong? Did I do something to offend you?"—all you got was a non-

committal "Nah, everything's okay." But you knew
it wasn't. There was a strange distance between
you that had never been there before.

Or maybe the relationship blew up in a single
instant, a sudden fight when hurtful things were
said, maybe even shouted. How quickly things can
change. The person you used to share everything
with doesn't even acknowledge you now when you
walk by.

One such friendship involved an incredible
musician who became a friend and mentor. We
attended the same church when I was a teenager.
He was a spiritual giant in my eyes as well as an
older "encourager." Eventually we moved away to
begin different lives in different cities. Over time, I
was shocked to discover that my friend's walk with
the Lord had slowed to a crawl. How he chose to
lead his life and how he failed to respond to my
phone calls told me what I hated to admit: He was
walking away from his first love.

Around that time I was getting my own spiritual act together. I certainly didn't feel judgmental;
when I moved from our hometown I took a few
detours myself. But I never got completely off

track. And I was never happier or more relieved
than when I finally saw the light and got things
right with God.

I wanted my friend to see that. I even wrote a
song on one of my first albums expressing my con-
cern for him. It backfired! He was angry and
chewed me out. How could I be judging him?

Fortunately things got better between us and
we've enjoyed each other's company—and music—
since then. But I know it may never be the same
between us and I continue to pray for his hunger for
the Lord. We were such good friends, "Bob" (not his
real name) and I. I really felt close to him, admired his
intelligence, his passion for the Lord, his spiritual gifts.
We were growing so close that we began working
together professionally. Our story proved the old
adage true: Never work with your best friend.

At the time, though, no one could have told me
that Bob and I wouldn't be the perfect business part-
ners. And things were great for a while. But when
circumstances changed in my professional life, I had
to make some tough decisions; Bob was deeply hurt
by the change that involved him. Amazingly, from
my perspective at least, it was the end of an era.

When our smooth-sailing friendship hit some major turbulence, it sank. It was like watching the Titanic go down. What had seemed invincible and built like a rock (because it was built on The Rock) crumbled—and fast. And although we have tried to repair it, our relationship remains broken.

In retrospect, I could have handled the situation better. For example, I was so embarrassed by the whole thing that I didn't follow up with him like I should have. I didn't sit down with him for many more talks to work things out. It was as hard for me as it was for him, and sometimes, when something gets that awkward, it's easier to just avoid it.

I'm normally a pretty good communicator, but this time my communication skills failed me. There were some painful misunderstandings that made a bad situation even worse. Plus, there was the constant guilt I felt—even though I believed it was unjustified guilt.

Obviously, my friend didn't see it that way.

Over the following weeks, then months, and now years, I have done everything in my power to keep our friendship going. I've confessed stuff that wasn't truly my fault, just to try to put things right.

I've told him, "Whatever it takes, man, I'll do it. Just tell me. What do I have to do to show you I want to keep you as a friend?"

"Things are fine, Michael, they're just different," he says. "They're not the same anymore."

I don't think things are fine, mainly because I miss the close relationship we once had. I've had to accept the fact that our friendship may never be what it once was. That happens sometimes. When a friendship is this fractured, is the relationship worth fighting for?

WHEN FRIENDSHIPS FALL APART

Drs. Les and Leslie Parrott, co-directors of the Center for Relationship Development at Seattle Pacific University, offer a five-step plan for dealing with fractured friendships.[1]

Step One: Count the Cost

The first thing to do when faced with a fractured friendship is to ask yourself if the relationship is truly worth saving. The Parrotts write, "An unhealthy relationship is not worth repairing if it forces you to compromise your values or under-mine your self-respect . . . If your friend is pres-suring you into something you want no part of, for example, and you stand by your convictions, a good friend will understand and respect that. He or she may even change as a result. If not, you're probably better off without such a destructive relationship."

If your friend starts "experimenting" with things you know aren't right, be careful. I lost some good friends in high school when they went off into the party crowd. The change happened slowly, but I knew what was coming when we got together on Monday and they were all talking about the par-ties on Friday night. I couldn't join in because I hadn't been there. I knew it was only a matter of time until our friendship cooled, and I was right.

Another reason to let a friendship go is if it's actually bringing you down. Some relationships can become unhealthy. Does your friend bring out the worst in you? String you along? Make you feel like you don't matter? Are you being manipulated?

"Carefully consider the price you pay for keep-ing your friendship alive. And if the cost is too high, make a clean break," the Parrotts advise. "If, on the other hand, your friendship is worth the cost of repairing and maintaining it—if it has redeeming qualities you value—you're ready for the next step."

Step Two: Make Meaningful Contact

Your goal at this stage is to get one message across: "Our friendship is important to me, and I miss seeing you. Is there any way we can resolve what stands between us?"

The best way to make contact depends on the relationship. It might be a letter. For some, it's a telephone call or an E-mail message. You might even put some "sugar" on it and send the message with some balloons, or in a card, or with flowers.

The Parrotts point out that at this point you're not trying to resolve the dispute. There's no need to get into the details or even to apologize. There will be time for that eventually, but now is the time to get things going. One warning, however: Do a gut check and make sure you aren't harboring any resentment or anger. It'll come out, and when it does, you'll wreck your reunion.

To release your anger, you have to enter the third stage: *forgiveness*.

Step Three: Forgive as Best You Can

Back in the eighties, Lewis Smedes came out with a book that opened many Christians' eyes to a new aspect of forgiveness. In *Forgive and Forget,* Smedes points out that the first person served by forgiveness is the one who does the forgiving. Bitterness eats us up inside far more than it affects the person we're mad at.

The Parrotts agree. "Getting even takes its toll, not only on the offender, but on the one seeking revenge as well . . . Forgiveness helps us as much or more than our offender."

Here's the point: When you sit and stew over how somebody has wronged you, is the person you're angry at really affected? They're probably listening to music, reading a book, talking with someone else, doing whatever they like to do—while you sit and pout and make yourself miserable. Holding a grudge is one of the best ways to wreck any sense of joy and happiness.

So how do you forgive? First, you've got to

accept that you share some of the blame. I could have handled things differently with the employee I mentioned before. I think he could have responded differently, as well, but I needed to face up to my part of the problem. The Parrotts warn, "If you are not open to seeing the other side of the story, you will never be able to approach your friend in a meaningful way. If you think the problems that are cooling down your friendship are totally and completely the fault of your friend, think again. The problems that plague a friendship are rarely 100 percent the other person's fault. If you keep this in mind, you will be well on your way to practicing forgiveness instead of trying to balance the scales."

In addition to accepting your share of the blame, forgiveness also means letting go. When Jesus said that we are to "turn the other cheek," he didn't add, "*if* the other person says they're sorry." Jesus knew what He was talking about, don't you think? He knew bitterness and hatred eat us up inside, so He urged us to let it go.

Don't expect such a letting go to be a one-time event, though. Sometimes you have to forgive someone a hundred times over. Memories creep back into your mind and you have to force yourself to say, "I've forgiven that. There's no point in dwelling on it any longer." Corrie Ten Boom, a woman whose family was hideously persecuted for helping to hide Jewish people during Nazi occupation, was once reminded of a specific wrong done to her by the Nazis. Rather than stew over the past hurt, Corrie responded, "I distinctly remember forgetting that."

We need to have the same attitude.

Step Four: Diagnose the Problem

After you've evaluated the relationship, made meaningful contact, and worked through the process of forgiveness, you can then move to the fourth step: honestly diagnosing what went wrong. The Parrotts point out, "Viewing things in black and white seems easier and more practical. But most of life—including our friendships—comes in shades of gray. And if you don't accept that, you miss out on a lot of relationships that might have been."

I had this problem with my good friend Jimmy Bloss when we went to Ft. Lauderdale during spring break with two girlfriends. We stayed with Benny

Key, who played in the group Truth. He came across some minor league baseball tickets and gave them to me. For some reason, I didn't want to go, so I gave my tickets to Jimmy and his girlfriend.

When Jimmy got to the game, the number of the ticket I had given him was called. He found out that if he could throw a ball from the mound into a hole cut through a giant piece of wood, he'd win the cash pot that had been accumulating.

On his first throw, Jimmy missed the entire board, even though it was almost as big as a barn. On the second throw his aim was straight, but short of the target. The third throw was perfect; it sailed right through the hole and the crowd roared.

Jimmy won the jackpot!

When he got back to Benny's house and told me what had happened, I figured Jimmy owed me half the pot. After all, I had given him the ticket, hadn't I? Jimmy didn't see it that way. How he'd come by the ticket didn't matter; he had won the money, and it was all his.

I never saw a dime of that money, but Jimmy and I remained friends. Looking back, I think asking for half was a ridiculous request anyway—I can't believe I ever expected something! And Jimmy might have been able to lessen the tension by flipping a ten spot my way. Instead, both of us thought "black and white" and never could come to an agreement. I wanted half, he wanted all of it, and neither of us was willing to compromise.

Years later, it seems ridiculous how big a fight we had over such a little matter—in fact, we both laugh about it now. But that's what black-and-white thinking does—it alienates friends. In ideal situations, friends will diagnose the problem together. Honestly discuss your concerns, but then when it's your friend's turn to talk, listen as carefully as you can. Put yourself in his or her shoes. You might even say, "Help me to see things from your perspective. How did you interpret what I said? How could I have said that differently?"

If you don't find out what went wrong, you can't "fix" the friendship, and the misunderstanding will come back to haunt you.

Step Five: Rebuild Respect

What if your friend did you wrong in the worst way? What if that person said something that hurt you as badly as you've ever been hurt? How can you ever relate to each other again?

The Parrotts suggest two things. "You begin by noting your friend's most admirable qualities. Ask yourself: What traits does he or she possess that inspire you to become a better person? Make a list of these qualities. If you're like most people, you may find yourself weighing these good qualities against the bad. That's okay. The point is not to whitewash your friend's personality. In fact, you may discover that he or she is simply deficient as a certain kind of friend. Some friends, for example, are great when you need a ride to the mall, but no help at all when you're in despair over a lost love. Once you know a friendship's limits, it's easier to enjoy it for what it is without feeling let down about what it's not. The goal here is to rebuild your respect by highlighting those qualities you like best about your friend."

The Parrotts also urge us to offer sincere apologies for what we have done wrong, specifically identifying things that were said or done about which we are sorry and need to ask for our friend's forgiveness.

Been there, done that. So what now? Despite all my best efforts, at least two of my best friends are still having a hard time letting me back into their lives. In fact, I've been wondering if there would ever come a time when we'd be together again—like old times. At least, I was wondering . . . until just a short time ago . . .

Survivors!

Like a well-written and orchestrated song—just the right balance of instruments and vocal, lyric and melody—I love it when all my relationships are running smoothly: Deb is happy and fulfilled, the kids feel loved and protected, and all of my friends know how special they are to me. In a perfect world, that's how it would be. But as you already know from this chapter's intro, that's not how it always is. Sometimes the music—sour notes, miscues, and all—comes to a screeching halt.

Something happened recently, though, that gave me the greatest hope for all kinds of relationships, including friends at church. Several years ago, Deb and I caught a vision for establishing a group of believers "passionately committed to worshipping Jesus, teaching His Word, and showing His love by serving and meeting the needs of others." This dream has come true as we have joined our hearts with others who have heard the same call.

But just like any other relationship in life, this one, too, has taken lots of patience and perseverance. We've had to learn as we go, how to work together to bring the greatest glory to God. And sometimes, even in the place where you'd think everything would be a little bit of heaven, there are challenges and tests of our love for one another and our patience with the process of becoming all that God wants us to be.

For one thing, our little fellowship is having growing pains. We're still experimenting with the right blend of praise and worship, teaching and preaching, giving and praying. And sometimes feelings can get hurt when gifts are not used or appreciated as much as they should be. So, in addition to everything else on my plate these days, I meet weekly with the leadership team of our church to pray and discuss ways of working out the kinks.

One week, because of some sticky scheduling

problems, I was dreading our meeting. We really needed to get some structure going and hold the line on running overtime. That's difficult to do when we really get into worship or when the preacher gets wound up.

I had agonized over how to approach one of my friends who plays a major role in leadership. He's incredibly gifted, so we didn't want to quench the work God is doing through him. And needless to say, I sure didn't want to say or do anything to hurt him. So I wrote a letter, praying every minute, asking God to let me express my heart, also praying that my friend wouldn't be offended, but receive the letter, and our comments, in the spirit in which they were intended.

Feel free to read over my shoulder:

Jim,

I'm here to tell you that I think you are doing a great job in your role at New River. Thank you for your heart for the Body. You have a tremendous amount of compassion, which I believe is a gift from God.

I would like to make a recommendation—that you would consider spending some time with Don

Finto. I believe he has great wisdom in regard to lead-
ing a congregation. He is passionate for the Lord like
nobody I have ever known. I believe you could learn a
great deal from him. The same for me; I could sit at
his feet for days. I strive to do the same for what God
has called me to do—to lead people into the throne
room of the Lord God Almighty. That is why I have
tons of worship CDs, and am always listening to new
material to see if someone has tapped into the heart
of God as it relates to worship.

I'm in process, like we all are, and only want to
be an encouragement to you as a brother and want
you to fulfill your destiny in what the Lord has called
you to do. I love you more than you will ever know.

Your friend for a lifetime,
Michael

After delivering the letter before the meeting, I
held my breath, waiting for his reaction. Would it
be like the friends I mentioned earlier? If so, my
well-meaning letter could cause anything from a
minor ripple in our relationship to a full-blown crisis in our church! You can imagine my relief—and

my gratitude to God—when I received this e-mail later that night.

> Brothers,
> Enjoyed our meeting tonight and thought we shared a lot of great and much-needed ideas. Thank each of you for speaking candidly into my life. You encouraged me and yet shared some points that will improve both my presentation and the hearers' ability to digest the Word. To me it was a classic example of our not worrying about offending each other, but speaking the truth in love and trusting each other with the counsel.
>
> Have a great rest of the week!
> Jim

I slept like a baby, drifting off to sleep with the sense that God's plan works. Friends can be friends forever if both parties are sold out to His principles. And fractured friendships can be repaired without a crack!

CHAPTER EIGHT

Winter-Spring Friendships

One of the greatest honors in my life came on June 13, 1994, when I played at the first Billy Graham event that featured rock and roll, rap music, and videos. I had played at some crusades before, but this was the first bona fide youth night, ever. This was a big departure for the Billy Graham Evangelistic

Association, and everybody was pretty nervous—except Billy! He was so calm and peaceful. When we saw the crowd of more than seventy thousand absolutely *pack* the Cleveland stadium, Billy told me, "Thank you for being here, Michael. You know they're all here because of you."

I said, "I don't think so." It was our only disagreement—and I know I was right on that one! The Billy Graham Evangelistic Association had asked me to perform "Secret Ambition." I sang the song in front of a 20-by-28–foot Jumbotron video, specially produced for the Graham crusade. And then, after my song, I was given the honor of actually introducing Billy Graham to the crowd.

That night, Billy delivered one of the best sermons I've ever heard him preach. He was certainly "on," and the response was flat-out amazing. I sat and cried as I watched ten thousand kids walk down the aisles to make a commitment to Christ.

Billy is an incredible man. He has become something of a mentor for me. We've gotten together at his home, he's asked me to participate in a number of crusades now, and we talk on the phone from time to time. Billy and Ruth love Deb so much; it's a good match. Though Billy is almost twice my age, we have a lot in common in terms of what we do—we both have five kids, our lives have involved a lot of travel, and we both have lived in the limelight.

It's always fun to go to the Grahams' house. Watching Billy and Ruth interact is a lesson in itself. The two of them are filled with spunk, so Deb and I always have a great time over there. In fact, it was because of Ruth that I've learned to eat with chopsticks. Ruth really likes Chinese food, but she won't ever let me use a fork. We always have to use the sticks—she can be very strong willed that way. My first attempts with the chopsticks were hilarious, but eventually I got used to them.

To be honest, I'm blown away that I even know the guy. When they write history books a couple of hundred years from now, you know Billy will be a big part of that. To consider this man my good friend is more than I can imagine.

When I talk about friends, I don't think just about people my age. In fact, most of the men I've considered my closest friends have all been one or even two generations older than me. I think I'm drawn to these men because of their wisdom. When somebody has walked with the Lord a long, long time, they've got answers that younger people don't.

You've heard me mention Don Finto several times in this book; he's now in his seventies, twenty-seven years older than me. Billy Graham is about forty years older. Bob Briner, another close friend who passed away a while back, was eighteen years older. I want to be around godly men who are veterans in the Lord, and it's paid off. Don Finto is very responsible for my marriage and for the way my kids are turning out. His influence has reached into every area of my life. I still have my "problems" and "issues," but they'd be a lot worse if I had never met Don.

WISE FRIENDS

Sometimes, younger people sell themselves short when they don't consider building friendships with older people. Maybe it all goes back to what Mick Jagger once said about trusting anyone older than thirty. I think that's making a big mistake. In fact, I'd go the other direction and say you're treading dangerous water if you don't have any friends in their fifties, sixties or seventies. Why? Because without older friends, the counsel you receive won't have perspective; it won't be based on time-tested experience.

Consider what happened to Rehoboam, Solomon's son. When Solomon died, the throne was passed to Rehoboam, which gave him, obviously, a lot of power. The Israelites came to Rehoboam and promised to follow him as king if he'd ease up a little bit on the heavy taxation that the people felt buried under. "Your father made our yoke heavy; now therefore, lighten the burdensome service of your father, and his heavy yoke which he put on us, and we will serve you," the people promised (1 Kings 12:4).

Rehoboam initially made a wise move here: he asked for three days to consider his decision. It's a good idea not to be too hasty, so Rehoboam gathered all his father's advisers together. These were wise men, time-tested and experienced.

He asked them, "How do you advise me to answer these people?" (v. 6).

They responded, "If you will be a servant to these people today, and serve them, and answer them, and speak good words to them, then they will be your servants forever" (v. 7). In other words, they said, "Lighten the load! Speak kind, gentle words, and you'll win their hearts."

Then Rehoboam turned to his younger friends, the guys he hung out with, and asked, "What advice do you give? How should we answer this people who have spoken to me, saying, 'Lighten the yoke which your father put on us'?" (v. 9).

The friends' newfound influence and power, coupled with their youth and inexperience, made them prideful, and they gave Rehoboam some different—and disastrous—counsel. They said, "Thus you should speak to this people who have spoken to you, saying, 'Your father made our yoke heavy, but you make it lighter on us'—thus you shall say to them: 'My little finger shall be thicker than my father's waist! And now, whereas my father put a heavy yoke on you, I will add to your yoke; my father chastised you with whips, but I will chastise you with scourges!'" (vv. 10–11).

119

Rehoboam had a clear choice to make: He could go with the wisdom of his father's counselors or he could listen to his young friends. Tragically, he went with the young guys, and as soon as the people heard Rehoboam speak these words, they left him. Rehoboam became the last king of the united monarchy in Israel; he lost what his father, Solomon, and grandfather David had worked so hard to build (vv. 12–24).

This isn't to knock young people, but I discovered pretty early on how valuable it was to listen to guys who had far more experience than I have. One such friend is Joe White, from Kanakuk camp. Joe's at least ten years older than me, but that has given him the ability to ask me the tough questions that younger friends might not think to ask. When Joe says, "How are you, Michael?" he isn't just making small talk. He means, "How are you *really* doing?"

Early in my career, I was struggling with learning how to say no to requests. The result was that I was too busy, and my family was suffering. Both Joe and Don Finto rode my case: "You can't do everything, Michael. It's okay to say no every now and then."

A younger guy might have advised me to go for

it, to take advantage of every opportunity. After all, I was young, and who knows how long the doors would be open? After all, there aren't many working pop singers in their fifties.

If I had followed my younger friend's advice, I might have lost my family and marriage and ended up in a terrible situation. Today, my career means nothing to me compared to my family—Joe and Don helped me learn that early on. Their experience told me I'd feel that way eventually, and they were right.

FAMILY FRIENDS

Sometimes, the best older friends are related to you. Another influence in my life has been Debbie's grandfather, A.V. Washburn. When he finally died in 1997, Debbie's mom, A.V.'s daughter, wrote an article in my newsletter, *Michael's Best Friend,* that I'd like to share with you here. It'll give you an idea of how much my life has been impacted by this incredible man.

To millions of Southern Baptists around the world, he was "Mr. Sunday School." To Kate, his wife of sixty-four years, he was "A.V." To Michael and Debbie and five other grandsons and granddaughters and their spouses, he was "Granddaddy." To 13 great-grandchildren, he was their beloved "Boompop." To me, he was simply . . . "Daddy"—the best in the world.

If A. V. Washburn hadn't been called to a teaching ministry that circled the globe, I think he might have been a musician. He always enjoyed music so much—especially Michael's—from rock to reverent. Something special went on between those two when Michael would sit at the keyboard, play some new melody or work-in-progress, and glance up for Boompop's reaction. Often, that reaction was misty eyes; sometimes, it was a knee-slap and hands clasped above his head in a victory sign. "Michael, that's the best thing you've ever done," he'd exclaim . . .

There was music in Daddy's life until the very end. For weeks, while he slept or stared out the window at the now-leafless trees, he listened to Michael's music—either on tape or live, when Michael would drop in to pray and play the synthesizer he kept at their house for impromptu concerts. Those hours brightened Daddy's last days and brought a little bit of heaven into his room.

So it shouldn't have been a surprise that it was while Michael was playing "Emmanuel"—this time on the Kathie Lee Christmas Special on television—that Daddy took his last breath—on the very final chord of that song! Through our tears, we saw on his face such peace—and the biggest smile—as if God were allowing us a glimpse of the glory Daddy must have been experiencing at that moment. And I'm sure, if we could have heard his heart, we would have heard him saying to Michael, "That's the best thing you've ever done."

A.V. was such a huge encouragement to me—as he was to everybody. He was probably my biggest supporter. Every time I played him a new song, he always told me, "Michael, that one is going straight to the top." He was convinced that every song I ever wrote was destined to be a number one single!

He had been very sick for a long time, so I

stopped by his house on my way to the airport before I left on a road trip. I played a couple of songs for him on the synthesizer, then caught a flight to Houston, where I was performing in a show with Amy Grant. I completed my part in the first half of the program and went backstage, where someone told me the Kathie Lee special, taped earlier, was on TV. I watched the special, but in the middle of my TV performance, I had to go back onstage to finish my live performance.

After that segment, somebody told me that Deb was on the phone. Her words were pretty simple: "Just wanted to let you know: Granddaddy passed away, but you're not going to believe what happened! He breathed his last breath exactly when you finished your last chord on 'Emmanuel!'"

I was absolutely blown away. I could not believe it. Some might think the timing of his death was a coincidence, but I don't. God works that way sometimes.

Amy's show wasn't over. I still had to go back onstage. She came in to tell me how sorry she was. The Katinas said the same thing: "Man, we're praying for you."

To be honest, it wasn't that big a deal to go back out onstage, and I'll tell you why. A.V. (since the kids called him "Boompop," we usually did too) had lost a lot of weight and become terribly thin; the cancer had really taken its toll. When I got back out there, I thought, *Boompop is probably dancing right now, having the time of his life in a glorified body. He isn't sick anymore.*

This made me want to worship all the more. Boompop was one of the most amazing men I've ever met in my entire life. He was so lovable; *everybody* loved Boompop. Whenever he walked into a room, he brought so much joy. Yeah, it was painful to realize that he wasn't going to be around anymore, and it hurt to know that Deb's grandmother wouldn't be with the man she loved. They had dated for six or seven years, and been married for sixty-four, so she really couldn't imagine life without him.

But all of us knew exactly where he was now— a good man, rewarded by his God, receiving his gift of heaven, and we rejoiced. Now that Boompop is gone, I'm even more thankful for every minute I got to spend with him.

STRETCH YOURSELF

I'd like you to stretch yourself—relationally. We need to have friends our own age that we can hang with, laugh with, even goof around with. But I hope you're not limiting yourself to only these types of friendships. I hope you're getting the positive and powerful influence of an older and wiser generation.

Recently, something kind of wonderful has been happening in my own life. Now that Rocketown Records is a reality, I'm becoming a father figure to some struggling young musicians. Now *I'm* playing the fatherly role, one of my goals is to mentor for a lot of young artists coming into this business.

Don't limit your friendships to people who are your age. Look around. Stretch yourself. The friend of a lifetime might be one or two generations older—or younger—than you!

CHAPTER NINE

Friends Who Don't Believe

efore there was my good friend and mentor Billy Graham, there was George Whitefield. He was to the eighteenth century what Billy Graham was to the twentieth—the most famous evangelist and preacher in the entire world.

Like Graham, Whitefield got an early start

in life, preaching throughout the American colonies when he was in his mid-twenties. Though George lived in England, his trips to America resulted in greater and greater notoriety, until he became what one writer describes as "America's first celebrity."[1]

Think what it must have been like to live in a time when the most famous person in the country wasn't an athlete, a singer, a politician, a movie star or a filmmaker, but a Christian. It's not that George didn't have his enemies—there were plenty of those—but as one historian puts it, "When [Whitefield] arrived in the colonies, he was simply an event."

Get this: stores shut down whenever George visited a town to preach. Farmers left their fields, and business virtually ceased as crowds flocked to hear the powerful evangelist. One sermon in Boston actually drew more listeners than the entire city's population!

No one gets this popular without being attacked, and Whitefield was no exception. He received death threats. Tough dudes tried to drown out his preaching by blowing horns. Even some members of the clergy, surprisingly enough, were among Whitefield's most vocal critics. They called him fanatical and intolerant—the same kinds of attacks that Billy Graham has faced throughout his career.

In the midst of this fame—and everything that goes with it—Whitefield set aside the time to build a close friendship with a guy named Ben. Ben was a self-made man, a "free thinker" and a skeptic. He was very successful, extremely inventive—downright brilliant. Though Ben believed in some form of God, he didn't buy into Christianity, calling it "idealistic fantasy." He was cynical, and when it suited him, promiscuous.

Even so, Ben found himself spellbound by the power of Whitefield's personality. He watched George face his detractors without flinching; he was impressed by Whitefield's logic, powerful persuasion, and obvious speaking skills; and he watched George long enough to know that this guy lived what he believed. Whitefield's was no fake. His faith was the real thing.

Because people listened to Ben, they wanted to know what he thought of the great evangelist. In his typical tongue-in-cheek style, Ben complimented

George while keeping his distance from what George taught. Here are just a few of Ben's comments:

"He can bring men to tears merely by pronouncing the word *Mesopotamia*.

"Never go to one of Mr. Whitefield's assemblies with money in your pouch, or you shall surely soon find it empty—such is his alluring power over the will of his listeners.

"There is hardly another minister of the Gospel alive who can so bring to life the truth and relevancy of the Scriptures. Almost, he persuadeth me to believe."[2]

Even more interesting, Ben bragged about George's skills as a friend, saying, "He is a fine conversationalist and a sympathetic listener. He is an ideal friend."

Because Ben knew everybody in town, the friendship proved as beneficial for George as it did for Ben. Ben published Whitefield's sermons and journals (which, by the way, earned Ben a ton of money) and kept in close contact with George through visits and letters for nearly three decades. In their book *Best Friends*, George and Karen Grant describe the relationship this way: "Over the course of nearly thirty years the two men carried on a vibrant correspondence and forged an intimate friendship that sustained them both throughout the rest of their lives. They encouraged one another. They stimulated one another. They inspired one another. They cajoled one another. And they comforted one another."[3]

Just before George died, he and Ben had been making plans to develop an experimental community that would explore how the principles of grace and freedom might be reflected in the real world. Though Ben didn't accept all that George taught, he clearly had enough respect for his friend to work side by side with him.

After Whitefield's death, Ben continued his friend's work, which eventually involved helping to found a new nation. George's influence on Ben became obvious, for during the Constitutional Convention in which America was born, Ben played a major role in helping the deadlocked delegates get on with their business. He suggested something quite surprising, coming from a well-known skeptic—that the delegates pray and appoint a Christian chaplain who would help them deal with their tensions in a more appropriate manner. It was after

Ben's earnest appeal and approval of the Constitution that the delegates finally voted unanimously to pass it.

By now you may have guessed that "Ben" was actually Benjamin Franklin, whom one historian calls "the first American." Because George Whitefield was willing to build a close and lifelong friendship with a non-Christian—and even an outspoken skeptic—he had a major impact on a country that was ultimately officially founded a few years after his death.

I think it's important for all of us to take the time to build and maintain friendships with nonbelievers. Jesus spent a good bit of His time eating with "sinners and tax collectors." Yes, we need the close friends who share our belief in God. But if we don't have any friendships with people who don't believe, how will we ever effectively impact our culture?

Friendship evangelism is the way we do it at Rocketown.

ROCKETOWN

I've written about this ministry before, but there's no way I can write a book about friendships without mentioning the great relational work that the staff at Rocketown is doing.

Rocketown is a downtown ministry and dance club that reaches out to today's kids. (For more information about Rocketown's ministry, look us up on the internet at www.rocketown.com.). At Rocketown, evangelism is all about relationships. Each volunteer is asked to pour his or her life into kids by establishing and nurturing a relationship with at least three other students. Our goal is not to build a Bible study or even a youth group. There's a place for that, but that's not what Rocketown is all about. Our purpose is to meet young people on their level—and on their turf.

For instance, over the years, one of our staff members was the Rocketown D.J., so his relationships focused on teaching three young guys everything he knew about being a D.J. Another guy was a break-dancer. He was incredible, and he had a skill that other guys wanted to learn, so that's what he focused on. There are skateboarders, would-be movie directors, guitar players, even mall rats (people who practically live at the mall). There are any number of artists—musicians, writers, photographers, painters, poets, philosophers—so we built an area called the Bridge, a fine arts studio, where we give lessons in painting, sculpting, and woodwork. There's also the Rock Quarry where local high school bands have the opportunity to record professional-quality demo tapes.

Cheri Hoffman, who works at Rocketown, explains it best:

> Kids today are hurting. They have heard so much talk about Jesus and yet seen so little of Him in the lives of believers that they have become disillusioned to the point of resistance. That's why the staff of Rocketown Ministries believes that the most important thing we can do for teenagers is not to tell them about Jesus, but to be Jesus to them . . . The first thing we do is love the kids where they are, no matter what the circumstances . . . While we love them, we look for a point of contact, an opening, something that will allow us to connect on a deeper level. Some take longer than others, but we inevitably find some common ground—skateboarding, music, sports, computers, whatever it is that lets us get to know them.

From then on, we build a long-term relationship that will earn us the right to speak. This
active relationship with an adult who is pursuing
a deeper walk with the Lord ultimately brings the
young person into the community of believers.

This process takes time. We may know
them for weeks or months before we ever speak
the name of Jesus. Throughout that time, however, we try to be living examples of His love,
reaching out to meet their needs. At any point
along the way, they might begin to ask questions, wondering why we care about them when
no one else does, or why we do the things we do,
or why our lives are so different from theirs.

Because of the relationship that has been
cultivated, we then have the ability to share Jesus
with them. They have already seen His love in
action, so they are more willing to hear about
Him. Once they understand and accept His love,
it then becomes their turn to "be Jesus" to someone else.

Everything at Rocketown is about creating
opportunities to build real friendships, so that ulti-

mately the students can develop the most important friendship of all—one with Jesus Christ. One young woman told a female staff member, "Thanks for giving my friend hope." We're as practical as possible. One young man was kicked out of his grandma's house and lived in his car for two weeks—in our parking lot! He was overwhelmed when he shared a real Thanksgiving dinner with a family that truly cared about him. Soon thereafter, he moved in with one of the volunteer staff members.

As you see, this isn't "contact" evangelism—"Listen to what I have to say in the next five minutes." There might be a place for that on some occasions. But the "contact" at Rocketown is all about caring. This is "let me share my life with you" evangelism. It begins by listening.

This type of faith sharing takes time. A young single mother debated against Christianity loudly and vigorously in our coffee bar for three weeks in a row until she finally gave her heart to the Lord. Her reasoning for surrendering to God? She said the Rocketown staff members were the "only people in my life who care about me."

It's one thing to have a dream about how something should be done, but it's more rewarding than you could imagine to see that dream actually happen. I knew my dream for Rocketown had come true when a boy told Shawn Hedegard, the current director, "If it weren't for Rocketown, I would have no friends."

Jason Noe, who used to work for Rocketown, once told his staff, "The requirement isn't cheap to work at Rocketown. It will cost a volunteer his or her life. A life of sacrifice, support, friendship, and love. This is the mark of a follower of Jesus; one person whose life has been changed by the love of God through a personal relationship with His Son, reaching out to touch another with the same quality of love. It is a love that respects and goes to all lengths to care."

This type of friendship evangelism was on center stage during the 1996 Grammys.

WINANS'S WAY

The family of a friend of mine celebrates Advent by doing special devotionals every Sunday in December. On the first Sunday they turned off all the lights. The house was completely dark, and one of the kids lit a candle. The smaller kids were surprised at how just one little match could illuminate everyone's face, which gave new meaning to the verse, "The people who walked in darkness have seen a great light" (Isa. 9:2).

CeCe Winans "lit a candle" at the 1996 Grammy awards. Debbie came to the ceremonies with me, and we were pretty pumped up. I actually won a Grammy that night so it wasn't hard to be in a good mood. But then we watched as one of the country artists sang an entire song with a steamy video playing behind him, complete with two women in unbuttoned denim jackets—and little, if anything, underneath.

Following him came another popular singer, who had a huge debut breakout album that year. Debbie wrote about this artist's performance in my newsletter, *Michael's Best Friend:* "I found myself cringing as she sang about oral sex and used the dreaded F-word—a discomfort clearly not shared by the audience, who cheered each instance of profanity."

That was the darkness. Next, Debbie describes how CeCe, a friend of mine, pierced that darkness.

Finally, the thrilling gospel segment. As CeCe Winans began to sing in her hauntingly beautiful voice, "I Surrender All," I could feel a stirring in the audience. It wasn't long before we were all on our feet as the choir joined her and the momentum built. This soulful rendition was followed by a duet with Whitney Houston, who gave a personal testimony in "Count On Me." A little later, Shirley Caesar belted out her own rousing number. For those moments, God was glorified with the very vehicle He has given to worship Him. Music in its purest, noblest form filled the auditorium, and I felt such gratitude and pride for the African-American roots of Christian music . . .

The crowning achievement of the Grammy night—covering the gamut of musical taste—had to be when CeCe received her award. I had to remind myself that this was not the Dove [Awards], because for all the world to see—and hear—God got a standing ovation that night! What a thrill to see my husband hand CeCe the Grammy for Best Contemporary Soul Gospel Album and then to see her beaming face, reflecting the joy of the Lord. And what an acceptance speech! I wish I had counted the number of times she used the name "Jesus." With a boldness straight from the throne of God, CeCe thanked the Lord for her gift of music and declared to the audience that He is the reason she sings . . . and lives.

She turned to Whitney Houston, who had peeked out from backstage to share this moment with her dear friend, and told the superstar that Jesus loves her and is working in her life. Then CeCe faced that massive auditorium packed with a captive audience and proclaimed the truth that Jesus loves them—every one of them. For that moment, at least, I believe they were convinced.

See what CeCe was doing? Not only did she provide a witness to the entire world, but she obviously had also made time in her life to build strategic friendships, like the one she has with Whitney Houston. The music business is full of all kinds of people. Rather than run ourselves into a Christian ghetto, we need to be like CeCe—befriending fellow artists, while still boldly proclaiming the gospel. Dietrich Bonhoeffer wrote, "The Christian . . . belongs not in the seclusion of a cloistered life but in the thick of foes. There is his commission, his work."[4]

ONE THING AT A TIME

In the late 1930s, Albert Einstein, who developed the theory of relativity, joined the Institute of Advance Study at Princeton University. The institute's founder loved golf and, like most people who love the game, encouraged everyone to give it a try—including Einstein. Albert never showed much interest, but finally got tired of being hounded and agreed to take a lesson.

He met with a young teaching pro. Imagine what it must have been like trying to teach the world's smartest man—the guy eventually chosen by *Time* magazine as the "Man of the Century"—how to hit a golf ball.

Unfortunately, while Einstein had an above-average mind, his hand-eye coordination wasn't the best. He kept missing the ball, or hitting it fat, or taking chunks out of the ground while barely moving the ball. After each miss, the young teaching pro dutifully explained what Einstein had done wrong and tried to correct it.

"Okay, Professor Einstein, try not to lift your shoulders this time.

"Take the club back slow and easy. Slow and easy.

"Don't grip the club so tightly. Hold it looser.

"You're jerking back on the downswing. Try to make it smoother."

As the lesson progressed, Einstein seemed to be getting worse, not better, and he was growing increasingly frustrated. After the pro gave yet another solution, Einstein finally asked the young man to give him several golf balls. The pro handed over four. The great physicist then said, "Catch!" and threw all four balls at once.

The pro missed every single one.

The professor explained, "Young man, when I throw just one ball, you can catch it. If I throw all four at once, you miss every one. So when you teach, make only one point at a time!"

I like to remember Einstein's advice when I'm talking to nonbelievers. For whatever reason, I've had a number of very successful men seek me out and share some of their concerns. The temptation many of us face in these situations is to try to solve all of a person's problems at once. Or, if they don't believe, we try to answer every single objection they might have about the faith.

Get real. If a person has problems believing in a God who sends people to hell, for instance, and also wonders if miracles ever happened, and then can't quite make himself believe in a virgin birth, it's not very likely that you'll overcome every objection in a thirty-minute talk. Many times, when we share our faith, less is more. Deal with issues as they come up, but understand you can't "fix" everything in a single conversation. True friendship means we're in it for the long haul. We may have to take part in a hundred conversations before somebody is willing to put his or her trust in God.

Making the Most of Every Opportunity

In the early nineties, a couple of hits, including "I Will Be Here For You" and "Place in This World," thrust me into the mainstream. Along with the increased record sales came the obligation to show up at parties to promote the record. I also went to a lot of radio stations for interviews, and the record company would send a representative down to accompany me.

The rep and I would end up in the car for half a day, eat lunch, and have a lot of time to talk. It finally dawned on me one day that I wasn't just there to promote a record—I was being given the opportunity to reach out to some people who would never set foot inside a church. I didn't hit them over the head with a heavy message, though. Instead, I just started asking questions: Are you married? Where'd you grow up? How many kids do you have? What brought you into the music business?

It was amazing how quickly we got into some serious issues. When you show an interest in other people's lives—an interest that nobody else, frankly, has ever shown them—it's amazing how quickly they open up. And then it's only a matter of time until they ask, "Well, what about you? What's your purpose in life?"

Not every one of these meetings has led to what I'd call a "friendship," though a few have. There are some people I met back then that I feel very compelled to stay in touch with.

Paul urges us to make "the most of every opportunity" (Eph. 5:16 NIV). I don't think that means we have to give the four spiritual laws to every person we happen to meet. But I do think it means we need to look for opportunities to build friendships and, out of those relationships, to share the gospel.

Is there a friendship you need to start building today?

PURE MOTIVES

Let me check myself here, in case some of you take these thoughts too far. I'm *not* suggesting that we "prey" on nonbelievers, develop friendships with them, and then drop them if they aren't interested in our faith. While the best thing we can do for a friend is to help him (or her) grow closer to God, we don't want to become what Paul Stevens calls "relational prostitutes" who discard their "friendships" with others as soon as it becomes clear that the other person isn't interested. That is absolutely the wrong approach; to win somebody over to Christ, we must have genuine love.

When kids come to Rocketown, they know what we're about, what our beliefs are, and where we're coming from. All of that is very clear up front. That kind of honesty and openness doesn't scare them away, because they feel genuinely loved. Many kids today desperately need a mentor and someone who will listen to them. Yes, we want to share our faith, but we're committed to them *regardless of their choices.* Dr. James Houston writes, "A true friend can never have a hidden motive for being a friend. He can have no hidden agenda. A friend is simply a friend, for the sake of friendship."[5]

I've built some solid friendships with nonbelievers, and I will be their friend until the day they die even if they never become a Christian. I'll be there for them because they're important to me. I don't see them as "targets" or "prospects." They're my friends, and I'm committed to them, regardless. Of course I'd love to see them know God's love, in part so that our friendship could continue through all eternity. But I'm not going to dump them if they don't immediately convert.

My real frustration with Christians in the year 2001 is that we have a lot of "Christian country clubs." We stay in our subculture, and I want to ask, "What happened to bringing the lost people in? How many unbelievers are we bringing to church?" The answer is, sadly, not many, because we've isolated ourselves from people who don't have a personal relationship with Christ.

We're missing out when we fail to build friendships with nonbelievers. In fact, whenever I'm establishing a relationship like this with someone who doesn't know Christ, there's always a feeling in my gut telling me, *This is what it's all about.* I don't want to be anywhere else in the entire world than right there with that radio guy in L.A. who's cussing up the world, but also talking about his family and asking serious and honest questions about spiritual things. The reason he's opening up to me is because I chose to come into his life on his terms; I'm just there to love and serve him.

I really believe that my greatest gift and asset going into the world is that I don't preach; instead,

I go out of my way to serve, and I've found that serving others is disarming for a lot of people. After a while, I know I've made a dent, seen part of that wall go down, and I know that I'll have a chance to share the gospel. It might take six months, but eventually serving others will open up the doors.

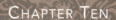

CHAPTER TEN

Keys to Friendship

Sometimes, I get in a big hurry. Especially if there's a mountain of fresh snow in front of me.

Back in high school, Joe Dorsey, Jimmy Bloss, and I went to Snowshoe, a ski resort in West Virginia. I was wearing a duck-yellow snowsuit. It looked cool back then, but I wouldn't be caught dead in it now!

The place was packed with people, and the three of us had decided we wanted to ski together, but it seemed like Joe and Jimmy were taking forever to get their boots on.

"I'll meet you guys down by the lifts," I said.

"Michael, if you wait just a few minutes we can go with you."

"Just meet me down there," I said, getting really impatient. "Go left at the lifts and I'll wait for you."

It was nine o'clock in the morning. The next time I saw them, it was five-thirty in the afternoon! They had gone left at the ski lifts like I told them to, but then there were three different directions to choose from. They chose a different one, and we never could find each other, so I spent the whole day skiing alone.

I was pretty ticked off—at myself, not at Jimmy and Joe. I felt like I had blown a whole day when I could've had fun with my two best friends, all because I didn't want to wait. It wasn't "convenient."

A big realization hit me when I was in my late twenties: It's not about me; it's about being a good friend. I stopped focusing on how others were treating me and started concentrating on how I was treating others. That change of focus did wonders for my ability to make and keep friends. In this chapter, I'd like to share some of the things I've learned about how to be a good friend.

A Friend Is Someone Who Gives

A century and a half ago, Emerson wrote something that has become almost a cliché today, but it's so true: "The only way to have a friend is to be one." The famous evangelist Dwight Moody put it this way: "What makes the Dead Sea dead? It is all the time receiving, but never giving out anything. Why is it that so many friendships grow cold? Perhaps it is because they too are all the time receiving, never giving."[1]

Let's be honest—almost all of us are too busy, so being a friend is never easy unless we're willing to give up something in order to have the time to act like a friend. God has a way of interrupting our "important plans" by putting people in our paths who need us to be there for them. These interruptions are never convenient, but they're the true test of how seriously we view our friendships. Are we willing to let our schedules slide in order to be there for someone?

I face this reality every day. I have a lot of friends and a busy life, and the two always seem to be running into each other. Just as I was working on this book, trying to meet the publisher's deadline, a close friend from high school committed suicide. I lost a lot of time dealing with this guy's tragic death and talking to other friends (including Joe and Jimmy), which delayed this book—but how could I write a book about friendship if I didn't take my own friendships seriously?

By giving, I don't just mean presents. Giving is an attitude. After someone spends time with you, what do they think about themselves later on? G.K. Chesterton once said, "There is a sort of great man who makes his friends feel small. But the authentic great man makes his friends feel great."[2] Do your friends feel great about themselves after they've spent time with you, or do they feel cut down, beat up, maybe even abused? When you're with them, are you thinking about how to build them up, or about how to build yourself up at their expense?

I had an opportunity to help a friend in 1992. Amy Grant, Wayne Kilpatrick, and I were all nominated for the Dove Song of the Year Award for our work on "Place in This World." Amy was in Europe during the award show, so when they announced our names as the winners, Wayne and I made our way up to the stage. Even though Wayne is an incredible songwriter, unbelievably talented, this was his first Dove Award.

No way was I going to take the spotlight. I gently pushed Wayne in front of me and made *him* do the talking! The crowd really helped. They realized that recognizing Wayne was way overdue, and jumped up to give him a standing ovation.

It was wild, and a lot of fun. Sometimes it's way more meaningful to let others enjoy the spotlight.

A Friend Works on Himself

As you know, Ben Franklin was one of the most famous men in his day. He served as the American colonies' ambassador to France, but he was also widely revered throughout America. One writer calls him "the most sought-after man in Paris."[3]

In short, Franklin was "the man." If you were throwing a party, Ben was the first guy you invited. If you wanted to sell a book, Ben was the person you'd ask to write the foreword. If you wanted to be known as cool, Ben was the guy you'd want to be seen with.

What's interesting, though, is that Ben wasn't always this way. In fact, for much of his early life he was an obnoxious loser. In his autobiography, Ben talks about how, as a young man, he walked around Philadelphia like he owned the place. He was full of his own opinions, quick to judge—the type of guy who just grates on your nerves.

One day an old Quaker friend finally pulled Ben aside and said, "Ben, you are impossible. Your opinions have a slap in them for everyone who differs with you. They have become so expensive nobody cares for them. Your friends find they enjoy themselves better when you are not around."[4]

Those were hard words—*Your friends find they enjoy themselves better when you are not around*—something I don't think any of us would ever want to hear, but these words hit Franklin hard enough to make him want to change. He decided to adopt an entirely different approach in his conversations:

I . . . dropped my abrupt contradiction and positive argumentation, and put on the humble inquirer and doubter.

I . . . forbid myself . . . the use of every word or expression in the language that imported a fixed opinion, such as *certainly, undoubtedly,* etc., and I adopted, instead of them, *I conceive, I apprehend,* or *I imagine* a thing to be so or so; or *so it appears to me at present.* When another asserted something that I thought an error, I denied myself the pleasure of contradicting him abruptly . . .

I soon found the advantage of this change in my manner; the conversations I engaged in went on more pleasantly. The modest way in which I proposed my opinions procured them a readier reception and less contradiction; I had less mortification when I was found to be in the wrong, and I more easily prevailed with others to give up their mistakes and join with me when I happened to be in the right.[5]

After months and then years of practicing this style, Franklin eventually lost the tag of "insufferable bore." Instead, he became the guy that everybody wanted to invite to their parties or to their homes for dinner.

You and I can make the same kind of change. We can look at the things we do that really turn people off, and decide to start treating them differently.

I had to do this with talking too much. I still occasionally struggle with it, but I think I'm getting better at keeping my mouth shut. I became sensitive to this, weirdly enough, by judging others—something I don't necessarily recommend you do! I'd see some guy who always wanted to steal the show and have everybody focus on him—the kind of guy who has an opinion about everything and is eager to tell everybody about it—and then I'd replay several of my own conversations and realize that in some ways, I was just like that guy! I had done most of the talking. I had shared all of my opinions, and I didn't have a clue what the other person thought concerning what we had talked about.

I decided to change. At meetings or after church or over dinners with friends, I kept thinking, *All right, Michael, be a better listener. Don't talk too much. Show an interest in them. Find out what they're thinking.*

Do you find yourself really bugged by some-thing that other people do? If so, that might be something that you struggle with yourself, and it may be something you should think about improv-ing. Teddy Roosevelt once said, "Don't worry about knowing people, just make yourself worth know-ing."[6] If we do this—work on ourselves instead of our friends—eventually we'll become the type of person other people will want to get to know.

A Friend Accepts You as You Are

A group of six friends were coming down from Snowshoe when we realized we were running low on gas, and nobody had any money with them. We had spent all our cash on skiing and food. I had a credit card with me, but back then, out in the mid-dle of nowhere, it was difficult to find a gas station that would accept credit cards.

To make things worse, we were really pressed for time. All of us had rented our skis, and if we didn't get them back to the shop in Kenosha by 4:00 P.M., we'd be charged for an extra day's rental.

We sweated it out until the inevitable happened and the van ran out of gas. It was really freezing outside; we had no money; we were in the middle of nowhere; and now we were stranded. Fortunately, an old pickup truck came by and gave us a lift to a gas station that accepted credit cards. We bought a can of gas, but the truck driver couldn't give us a ride back, so the six of us actually crammed into a police cruiser to get a lift to our car.

Along the way, the policeman got a call. He hit the lights and started doing eighty miles an hour, so we got to our car real fast!

We made it back to Kenosha on time—with twenty minutes to spare.

I think back to those times. There were six of us, we didn't have any money, and we couldn't even get a ski rack to stay on a car roof. What was the matter with us? But those friends, faults and all, gave me some of the best times of my life.

Every friend we make will have his or her shortcomings. Every friendship will face crazy times, frustrating times, and maybe even scary times. Friendships aren't always fun, but a true friend always accepts you as you are—bad breath, bad hair days, whatever.

In their book *Best Friends,* George and Karen

Grant write, "There are no perfect friendships because, alas, there are no perfect people. All of us have irritating habits, idiosyncrasies, wants, dispositions, proclivities, manners, demeanors, and quirks. Our friends must of necessity bear with us in charity and patience. They must have generous forbearance. Likewise, we must reciprocate. Through the ages, the best friendships have not been those where men and women have been especially well-suited, one toward another, but where they have been especially well accredited, one toward another."[7]

A Friend Is Someone Who Listens

In his bestselling book *The Man in the Mirror*, Patrick Morley tells about a time that a friend came to see him. "I just need someone to talk to," the man explained, then immediately started talking, kept talking, and never really stopped talking for an hour and a half. Finally, he stood up. "Thank you, Pat, you have no idea how much this has meant to me," and left.

Pat was surprised, saying, "All I did was say 'hello' and 'good-bye.'"[8]

Sometimes, saying "hello" and "good-bye"

between active bouts of listening is all a person really needs to do. It was said of Teddy Roosevelt, "Though a brilliant, humorous, high-powered talker, he was more ear than mouth. On the slightest indication that another had anything to contribute, he would jam on all his verbal brakes. He was perhaps the most creative listener I have ever encountered."[9]

After every concert I have kids who come up to me, and more than anything else, I think they just want someone who will listen to them. Their parents might be too busy; maybe they're too scared to talk to their youth pastor, and what they really want is someone who will hear them out.

Dietrich Bonhoeffer said that the beginning of love is to listen. "Just as love to God begins with listening to His Word, so the beginning of love for the brethren is learning to listen to them."[10]

One of the best ways to be a good friend is simply to listen, even if you can't offer any advice in response. In fact, sometimes it's better to bite your tounge and tune in to what the other person is saying. When we really listen to someone, we show we care.

Bonhoeffer warns, "He who can no longer listen

to his brother will soon be no longer listening to God either; he will be doing nothing but prattle in the presence of God too. This is the beginning of the death of the spiritual life, and in the end there is nothing left but spiritual chatter and clerical conde-scension arrayed in pious words."[11]

Instead of always trying to be right, learn how to listen. Instead of always wanting to be under-stood, learn how to understand.

A Friend Challenges You Directly Instead of Gossiping to Others

In the early years of the Revolutionary War, things weren't going so well for the colonies' gen-eral, George Washington. Though today we think of Washington as almost a mythical character, a truly great man, at that time many thought he was a loser who couldn't possibly win the war. People started gossiping and questioning Washington's leadership behind his back.

A true friend doesn't do that. He doesn't talk to others. He does exactly the opposite: he goes to the person involved and no one else. That's what Colonel Joseph Reed did with Washington, writing him a letter and speaking frankly about his concerns regarding Washington's leadership.

Rather than getting upset, Washington welcomed Reed's letter as a true act of friendship: "The hints you have communicated from time to time not only deserve, but do most sincerely and cordially meet with my thanks. You cannot render a more acceptable service, nor in my estimation give a more convincing proof of your friendship, than by a free, open, and undisguised account of every matter relative to myself or conduct."[12]

Do you have a friend who isn't really helping himself or herself, but who is turning others away, acting obnoxiously, ruining his or her own life? If so, don't say a word about it to anyone else. Go to your friend directly, and show that you care.

If you *have* to talk to someone, talk to God! Paul Stevens, an author and Regent College seminary professor, tells about the time his wife was on a canoe trip when she was a teenager. Two of the girls in the group kept criticizing a third, until the camp counselor asked them, "Have you ever considered that God has given us a spirit of discernment not to criticize but to pray?"[13]

When we see something that's not right in another person's life, there are only two people we should talk to about it: that person and God.

A Friend Lays Down His Life for You

Some years ago, *National Geographic* carried a powerful story about the aftermath of a forest fire in Yellowstone National Park. As forest rangers combed the mountainside to assess the fire's damage, one ranger saw a bird literally petrified in ashes, perched stone-like on the ground at the base of a tree. The sight of the now-charcoal bird made him queasy, and he knocked it over with his stick.

That's when he saw the movement.

Three tiny chicks scurried out from under their dead mother's stiffened wings. Apparently, the mother bird knew instinctively what to do to protect her children. Toxic smoke rises, so she gathered her babies at the base of the tree. She couldn't carry the chicks to safety. Though she could easily have flown to safety herself, instead she made the ultimate sacrifice, spread her wings over her babies, and stayed there—even as the heat of the fire ripped into her feathered body.

As one pastor reminded me, this is the same care God provides for us. Psalm 91:4 tells us, "He will cover you with His feathers, and under His wings you shall take refuge."

Unfortunately, some people don't enter friendships to lay down their lives for you—they enter "friendships" to use you. This motivation was pretty obvious when I toured with Amy Grant. Some fans tried to get her attention so they could take advantage of her. When I suspected that this was happening, I tried to protect her. A good friend will run "interference" at times like that. That's one way to "lay down our lives" for a person.

If you can do these six things—*be a giver, work on yourself, learn to listen, accept others as they are, talk to your friend directly instead of gossip, and learn to lay down your life for someone else*—you'll master the art of friendship. None of these skills are easy; few come naturally. But if we work on them, we *can* become better friends.

FRIENDSHIP BEGINS AT HOME

Wow! How could I have written a whole book on friendship and failed to stress my built-in support system—my wife, Debbie, and five junior Smiths? Oh, I've talked about them off and on for the past nine chapters, but maybe it wouldn't hurt to put in a word here. You know, some of your best friends are right under your nose—at home. And they deserve to have at least the same "friendship formula" in operation. By now, you know it by heart: *be a giver, work on yourself, learn to listen, accept others as they are, talk to your friend directly rather than gossip, and learn to lay down your life for someone else.* Sounds like a tall order, one that will take some effort.

The fact is I'm getting ready right now to go on a trip with my son Ryan, who's one of my very best buds. We play guitar together on tour occasionally, discuss his favorite topic—movies and books—by the hour (Dad making sure not to come on too strong as the conscience cop, yet sharing a few tips from the "older generation"), and even catch a flick when a really good one comes along. I expect to get in some practice on my friendship skills during this little father-son getaway. Like this one, for example: *What can I give Ryan that money can't buy?* Time. Kodak moments.

Then there's my lovely teenage daughter,

Whitney. I love it when we go out on "dates." Quiet and reserved, Whit opens up like a rose when we're one on one. I think she kinda likes her ol' dad and doesn't think it's un-cool to be seen with him. Our last date was the Father-Daughter Dance at school. She was the prettiest girl there by far! I just want to hang on to these great memories . . . she'll soon be dancing into some other man's life, much sooner than I care to think about. I intend to *work on myself* to keep Whitney coming home to Daddy!

Tyler is our athlete, and I'm told he looks the most like me of all my kids. He's into football and basketball and snowboarding. I honestly think there's not a sport he wouldn't try—kinda like his dad. Throwing the football around with him takes me back to my high school days. Tyler tackles life with the same kind of passion, although it's a quiet passion, whether it's art or video games or producing home movies. Go, Tyler! He doesn't talk much, but with so many talkers in the house, it's refreshing to be around Ty, and it's neat to *accept him just as he is*—the way my heavenly Father accepts me.

Our Anna may be the first woman president or the next female astronaut. She's unstoppable! She loves animals, friends (where have I heard *that* word before?), cooking with Mimi, and cross-stitching with Nana. But she always saves time for her dad. I'll never forget watching her dance when she was about four. She looked like a little princess, twirling in her make-believe world. Anna is one of those talkers I mentioned, but I love *listening* to her—whether she's yakking about what happened at school or playing the piano or sharing secrets. We keep close. We always will.

Emily is our "angel waiting for wings." And she's a riot! She can crack me up with one blink of those long lashes and her latest "funny face." If she isn't on horseback, she's dreaming about horses or drawing horses. The only way I could compete would be to audition for a rerun of that old sit-com *Mr. Ed*. Since she's the youngest, it's a little hard for me to rain on Emily's parade, but true friends *talk to each other* if something needs correcting. So as her dad as well as her friend, I try to balance our fun and games with some good old-fashioned "discipline," which interestingly enough, means "reining in." Sometimes I have to say, "Whoa, Em!"

You know, whether it's friends at home or

otherwise, the secret to keeping relationships alive and well is communication. Tons of it. None of the tips we've mentioned in this book will pay off if we don't stay in touch. And with all the balls I juggle everyday, I couldn't have handled the last twenty years of my life without Deb.

Tiny as she is, my wife Debbie is all the "girl" friends I ever had all rolled up into one. The first time I saw her, I was gone . . . and I still am. She's the one who inspired "Cross My Heart," which promises her that I'll stick around for the rest of our lives," "I Will Be Here for You," and "The Other Side of Me." Interestingly enough, though, the song that really captures what I feel for Deb was written by another guy—Jim Brickman. I recorded it on his album and the title speaks volumes in only five short words: "The Love of My Life." (But this is no place to replay our love story. Check out my book, *It's Time To Be Bold,* for the full scoop.)

As her husband, God has assigned me to be Deb's bodyguard, her covering. If we were facing war, it would be easy to take a bullet for her. What's not so easy is the day-to-day. Yet when I think about *laying down my life* for Debbie Smith . . . well, this is

where I get misty-eyed (yeah, guys do that too!)—
then all the little ways I can protect her are suddenly
a snap. Like taking out the garbage or driving the
kids to school . . .

Hey, I gotta go. It's Valentine's Day, and I've got
a romantic evening planned with my best friend!

*It Wouldn't
Be Worth It
Without Friends*

I hope you win, Chris."

"No, man, I hope *you* win."

Chris Rice and I were both up for the Male Vocalist of the Year Dove Award in 1999. Since he was a part of Rocketown Records, we saw each other a lot, and it became sort of a weekly ritual for us to see each other and trade the words, "Hope you win!"

"No, hope *you* win!"

Shortly after we started the Rocketown label, we received a copy of a custom record that Chris had cut, so we asked him to come in and meet with us. When he played "Welcome to Our World," we were blown away.

"If he's writing songs like this," I said, "who knows what the other songs will be like?"

Chris is far more than a musician, however. His personality is incredible. He doesn't have aspirations of being a star. In all honesty, he'd probably rather hang around youth groups than go play a show. We all love that about him! He's a poet who is extremely transparent, bares his soul, and isn't afraid to ask tough questions in his music. It's hard to pin down his music style, because I really believe he's got his own unique thing going on, but sometimes he reminds me of James Taylor. Who would have guessed that a guy with the depth of a James Taylor would succeed so wildly in a pop-oriented world? But Chris has, and I'm really happy for him.

We saw each other backstage right before the

show and went through the same ritual, this time for the last time: "Hope you win, man."

"Ah, no, I want you to win."

I was scheduled to perform "Live the Life" just before the male vocalist award was given out, and got the shock of my life when I was introduced by Gavi Lopez, a young woman from Ecuador my family sponsored through Compassion International up until the time she graduated from high school. It was great seeing Gavi there.

Since I was already backstage, I stayed there as they read through the names of the guys nominated for Male Vocalist of the Year. When they called out Chris's name, I jumped up and ran onstage, hugging Chris, honestly more pleased for him than if I had won it myself. I really did want Chris to win.

Later that night, one of the awards that I was fortunate enough to win was Artist of the Year. All my kids were there, watching in a suite with my parents at the Gaylord Entertainment Center. Deb grabbed and squeezed my hand when they called my name. What made the night really special, though, was seeing Chris get his award, hugging my family afterward, and getting to share some time with Gavi.

I'd be lying if I said I didn't care at all about winning Artist of the Year. I had been nominated a few times before, but had never won, so it meant a lot to me. But all of it wouldn't have been worth a dime if I didn't have my family, Chris, Gavi, and others to share it with. I really mean that. Friendships are what make life worth living.

I want to stress this because the music business in particular has a lot of very ambitious people who will use you, manipulate you, and try to leverage their own careers on your back. Maybe that's why some of our closest friends aren't even in the same business! Late at night, I feel sorry for people who are that ambitious, because even if they succeed, they'll find out that any success is pretty empty if you don't have someone to share it with.

If you never accomplish much of anything by the world's standards, but have a lot of deep friendships, you're a rich person. If you win three World Series championships, two Olympic gold medals, and record a couple of double-platinum albums, but die alone and unloved, you've lived a sad life indeed.

Think about where you spend your time, where you put your effort. Is it on other people? Or are you always thinking about yourself? Are you so busy with your own dreams that you can't get excited about helipng others fulfill theirs?

I'm telling you, friendship is where it's at. The tough times. The neon-sign, Fourth-of-July terrific times. The everyday-boring-same-old-same-old times. Try it. Try being a forever friend. And don't forget—whoever you are, wherever you live, you can count on me. *I will be your Friend!*

Notes

Chapter 1

1. Paul Stevens, *Disciplines of the Hungry Heart* (Wheaton, IL: Harold Shaw Publishers, 1993), p. 101.
2. Ibid., p. 113.
3. Ibid., p. 114.
4. Cited in George and Karen Grant, *Best Friends* (Nashville, TN: Cumberland House, 1998), p. 88.
5. Jerry and Mary White, *Friends & Friendship* (Colorado Springs, CO: NavPress, 1982), p. 13.
6. Cited in Grant, *Best Friends,* p. 42.
7. Stu Weber, *Locking Arms* (Sisters, OR: Multnomah, 1995), p. 22.
8. Dietrich Bonhoeffer, *Life Together* (San Francisco: Harper and Row, 1954), pp. 19–20.

Chapter 2

1. Weber, *Locking Arms,* p. 78.
2. Ibid.
3. Ibid., p. 81–82.
4. Ibid., p. 87–88.

Chapter 3

1. Weber, *Locking Arms,* p. 236.

2. Cited in Grant, *Best Friends,* p. 38.

3. James Houston, *The Transforming Power of Prayer* (Colorado Springs: NavPress, 1996), p. 227.

Chapter 4

1. Alan Loy McGinnis, *The Friendship Factor* (Minneapolis: Augsburg, 1979), p. 9.

2. Ibid., pp. 22ff.

3. Ibid., p. 24.

4. Cited in *A Treasury of Friendship,* compiled and edited by Ralph Woods (New York: David McKay Company, Inc., 1957), p. 90.

5. McGinnis, *The Friendship Factor,* p. 30.

6. Ibid., p. 34.

7. Katherine Anne Porter, "The Necessary Enemy," *The Collected Essays and Occasional Writings of Katherine Anne Porter* (New York: Delacorte, 1970), pp. 182–84.

8. Cited in Grant, *Best Friends,* p. 157.

9. Cited in *A Treasury of Friendship,* p. 341.

10. McGinnis, *The Friendship Factor,* p. 59.

11. McGinnis, pp. 76-77.

Chapter 5

1. White, *Friends & Friendships,* pp. 56–57.

2. Ibid., p. 91.

3. Cited in Grant, *Best Friends,* p. 62.

4. Bonhoeffer, *Life Together,* pp. 26–27.

5. Ibid., p. 28.

6. Ibid., p. 92.

7. Ibid., p. 93.

8. Cited in Grant, *Best Friends,* p. 163.

Chapter 6

1. Cited in Grand, *Best Friends,* p. 25.

2. Ibid., p. 28.

3. Weber, *Locking Arms,* p. 33.

Chapter 7

1. Dr. Les and Leslie Parrott, "What to Do When Relationships Fail," *Psychology for Living,* Sept./Oct. 2000, pp. 3ff. You can visit the Parrotts on the Web at www.Realrelationships.com.

Chapter 9

1. Grant, *Best Friends,* p. 50.

2. Ibid., pp. 55–56.

3. Ibid., p. 56.

4. Bonhoeffer, *Life Together,* p. 17.

5. Stevens, Cited in *Disciplines of the Hungry Heart,* p. 105.

Chapter 10

1. Cited in Grant, *Best Friends,* p. 104.

2. Cited in ibid., p. 160.

3. McGinnis, *The Friendship Factor,* p. 16.

4. Ibid., pp. 16–17.

5. Ben Franklin, *The Autobiography of Ben Franklin* (Roslyn, NY: Walter J. Black, Inc., 1941), pp. 25–26.

6. Cited in Grant, *Best Friends,* p. 64.

7. Ibid., pg. 119.

8. Patrick Morley, *The Man in the Mirror* (Grand Rapids: Zondervan, 1997), p. 157.

9. Cited in Grant, *Best Friends,* p. 92.

10. Bonhoeffer, *Life Together,* p. 97.

11. Ibid., p. 98.

12. Woods, *A Treasury of Friendship,* p. 356.

13. Stevens, *Disciplines of the Hungry Heart,* p. 106.

*Don't Miss
These Books by
Michael W. Smith*

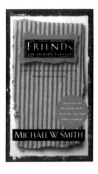

FRIENDS ARE FRIENDS FOREVER

This book looks beyond Michael the musician to present a man who relies on Scripture to provide him with daily guidance. "I'd like to tell you a few stories from my life—some wrong roads I've traveled, some right decisions I've made, and how God has often taken my mistakes and turned them into something good," Michael writes. In addition to his personal narratives, this book is filled with Scripture promises addressing such vital topics as faith, perseverance, loneliness, temptation, forgiveness, acceptance, and comfort.

ISBN 0-7852-6830-8 * Hardcover * 256 pages

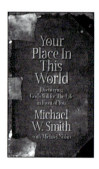

YOUR PLACE IN THIS WORLD

Ask Michael W. Smith to describe his role in the Christian community, and he'll tell you that he is an encourager. "Place in This World," his first breakthrough hit to cross over from contemporary Christian to mainstream popular music, expanded his horizons as he brought a message of hope to people unused to hearing such good news on Top 40 stations.

In *Your Place in This World,* Michael expands that message of encouragement with a series of never-before-told personal stories, reflections on Scripture, and thought-provoking insights from his friends. Through reading this book, you will find help in discovering your purpose, your passion, and God's plan for your life.

ISBN 0-7852-7020-5 * Hardcover * 224 pages

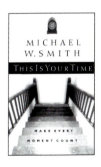

THIS IS YOUR TIME

For Michael W. Smith, 1999 was a tough year. It painfully reminded him that there is a time to die, a time to weep, and a time to mourn. Michael grieved with the parents and students at Columbine High School, mourned the passing of professional golfer and friend Payne Stewart, and faced the heartache of losing his mentor and friend Bob Briner. Instead of being depressed and feeling defeated over these losses, though, Michael was encouraged and challenged to live a more purpose-driven life. Each of us faces a moment when eternity whispers into our hearts, "This is your time." *This Is Your Time* calls readers to live their lives with greater passion for God and unwavering determination to make an impact on their world.

ISBN 0-7852-7035-3 * Hardcover * 192 pages